Daddy's
Prisoner

Daddy's Prisoner

ALICE LAWRENCE with
MEGAN LLOYD DAVIES

POCKET
BOOKS

LONDON · SYDNEY · NEW YORK · TORONTO

First published in Great Britain by Simon & Schuster UK Ltd, 2009
A CBS COMPANY

7 9 10 8 6

Simon & Schuster UK Ltd
1st Floor
222 Gray's Inn Road
London WC1X 8HB

www.simonandschuster.co.uk

Simon & Schuster Australia
Sydney

A CIP catalogue record for this book
is available from the British Library.

ISBN: 978-1-84739-807-9

Typeset by M Rules
Printed by CPI Cox & Wyman, Reading, Berkshire RG1 8EX

To my mum, my children and my big brother

CONTENTS

CONTENTS

PROLOGUE

I turn on the grill before bending to open the fridge door. Tea is going to be late tonight because we've been in the park for too long. I know I should be getting the children into bed because school starts early tomorrow but it was such fun watching them play – Emma and Lily laughing as Tom chased his ball. I didn't have the heart to force them all back indoors when I knew they were enjoying the fresh air. Now at last we're back home and the girls have had some yoghurt to keep them going until their food is ready. Tom, though, doesn't want to wait and wraps his arms around my legs as I pull the sausages out of the fridge and put them on a baking tray.

'Hungry, Mummy,' he says as I slide the food under the grill.

'Oh, baby boy,' I murmur. 'It won't be long now.'

Bending down, I kiss Tom on the top of his hair – so soft, it smells almost sweet – before picking him up and carrying him into the lounge. The girls are playing and the TV is blaring in the corner as I walk towards it. The news is on but even so I know there'll be trouble when I turn the volume down. I smile to myself as I bend down. Why are kids so addicted to TV these days?

A face appears on the screen as a voice starts speaking: 'An Austrian man has admitted imprisoning his daughter in a secret dungeon for twenty-four years.'

My hand freezes in space.

'Josef Fritzl has told police he fathered all seven of his daughter Elisabeth's children.'

I can't breathe. My head rushes.

'Police have confirmed that Miss Fritzl became pregnant six times during her imprisonment. One baby died soon after she gave birth to twins, three children were brought up by her parents after her father claimed she had abandoned them and three remained with her in the dungeon underneath an anonymous suburban home in the Austrian town of Amstetten.'

My legs tremble as I step backwards. My body feels heavy. Tom's arms are around me but I can't turn my head to look at him. I want to. But I can't.

I see a photo of a man on the screen. Grey hair and moustache. Unshaven. Blue eyes. Dead eyes. Just like the ones which kept me prisoner for so long.

Pictures flash into my head. The key turning in the front door. Windows nailed shut. Knives and guns gleaming in his cabinet.

I try to breathe.

Elisabeth. Her father. Six pregnancies. Just like me. Six children who survived. Not like me. My heart turns as I think of Jonathan and Caitlin.

Elisabeth was in a dungeon? At least I felt fresh air on my face sometimes, even if he was watching me every minute. I had glimpses of life, even if I couldn't live it before being locked back up again.

'Mummy?'

I look up. Lily is standing before me.

'Are you okay, Mummy? You look funny?'

'I'm fine, darling,' I whisper as I pull her to me. 'I just need a cuddle.'

Emma runs over and I wrap my arms around my children, trying to forget the pictures crowding into my head as I feel their warmth against me.

'He's gone now,' I whisper to myself over and over again. 'You made sure he left.'

But my body won't listen. My breath is ragged, my heart thudding as I hold on to the girls and their brother.

I wasn't the only one.

There was another man like my father.

Another daughter like me.

Elisabeth.

CHAPTER ONE

Much of my past has been locked away so deep inside that I am scared of setting it free; so many memories packed tight into the tiniest, darkest corners that I am afraid to let go. It feels as if I'm standing on the edge of the sea with the tips of the water curling over my toes, all the time knowing a wave could crash over me at any minute if I remember too much. When you've seen hell, you learn ways of forgetting so that you can quickly escape when you're taken back there in your dreams.

But I can't keep the past locked up for ever and, by telling my story, I hope to show that monsters don't always live in fairytales and things which happen in news pages aren't always a world away — they can be just around the corner. I spent years locked in flats and houses on streets which looked just like any other. Sometimes I was even allowed out into the real world but iron bars are not the only kind of prison. I wasn't hidden in a tower dreaming of a prince to rescue me but an ordinary someone who would reach out to help a person I'd been taught to believe was worse than worthless. A nobody, a shadow, a freak.

Much of what I can remember from when I was a child is broken into pieces and it's hard to put a date and time on it.

But I can remember pointers – whether my younger brothers and sisters were babies or toddlers, for instance – which help order my memories. The earliest one I have is of a Christmas when my younger sister Laura was about one. That means I must have been around six, my older brother Michael was eight and little Simon was five.

It had taken a while to get used to having a sister because my brothers and I had been on our own together so long. Before Laura arrived with us, we'd been told once before that we were going to have a brother or sister and had got excited as we tried to choose a name. All us kids were named after someone special like relatives or the musicians and actors that Mum loved.

But after we'd thought up names for the new baby and watched Mum's tummy grow bigger, she disappeared one day and came home empty-handed. She didn't look like Mum any more and her face was white as a ghost's as she told us the baby was being looked after by the doctors. All I could do was silently wonder what had happened because no one mentioned our brother or sister any more. When I was older, Mum told me she'd had a boy who was stillborn and it was her fault because she'd been stupid and moved furniture. But she didn't look me in the eye when she told me and by then I knew enough not to be sure I could believe her.

So I didn't know what to think when Mum told us once again that she was having a baby. Would she really bring a brother or sister home this time? She did – a baby girl called Laura – and, after two brothers, I loved having her to play with. Even though I was little, I liked helping Mum out with the baby and as Christmas approached the year after she was born, I got excited thinking about Santa Claus.

We didn't have many toys and most of what we did have were things for the boys like plastic soldiers and cars. However, a few weeks before Christmas I'd seen an advert for a doll's house with pink walls, flowered curtains and furniture in every room. My heart was set. The year before I had been given a Barbie doll which hadn't come in a shiny box like the ones I'd seen in shops. But I loved her anyway and if she had a beautiful house to live in then Laura and I could play with it.

'I must be a good girl,' I told myself night after night. 'Because then maybe I'll be given the doll's house.'

When I told Mum what I wanted, she said I should write a letter to Santa Claus.

Maybe I can make Daddy smile and laugh, I thought to myself as I wrote. Then Santa Claus will know I've been good.

Of course, even then I knew our Christmases were not like other people's because I'd heard girls at school talking about trees and turkeys, which we didn't have. But even so I hoped for the doll's house and waited patiently for weeks, dreaming of it every night. When the day finally came, Michael and Simon opened their presents to find they'd each been given a cap gun, sheriff's star and hat. We all knew Dad liked such things because he had a shield with real knives sticking out of it hanging on the wall and that meant the boys had to like those things too. But as my brothers looked at their presents, they started squabbling over one of the guns and suddenly I heard a crack. My stomach swooped.

'You've broken it, you little bastard,' Dad shouted as he lunged at Michael.

My brother flew off his feet as my father's hand smashed into him and I lifted up baby Laura to run behind the sofa, which was where we hid when Daddy got angry. Crouching down, I could hear Michael starting to cry. We just had to be quiet and then we would not get into any more trouble. Hearing another crack, I held on to Laura as Dad snapped the damaged gun clean in two and threw the bits across the room.

'Do you like it now, eh?' Dad yelled at Michael. 'No fucking gun any more for you, is there? Your brother can have what's left.'

I waited until the room was finally quiet again before crawling out from behind the sofa. Dad was watching the TV. The argument was over. My brothers and I looked at each other. Now maybe I could have my present and my heart beat hard as Mum put a small package into my hand.

I stared at it. It was small, not the size of a doll's house at all, and I ripped open the paper to see a brooch which I recognised from Mum's jewellery box. It had a lady's face in cream on it with a beige background and, even though I knew I shouldn't, I started crying as I stared at it. All I could think of was the doll's house. I couldn't stop my tears as I thought of the Barbie doll lying on our dirty carpet when she could have been living in a beautiful house.

'Stop your blubbing,' Dad yelled as he turned his head to look at me. 'You can't always get what you want.'

I stared up at him.

'You'll get what you're given,' Dad screamed, his eyes darkening. 'Now fuck off out of here.'

I walked towards the door, holding the brooch in my outstretched palm. Behind me, I could hear Dad grumbling as I turned the door handle and he called my name.

'Alice?' he hissed, and I turned to look at him. 'Don't you realise there is no fucking Santa Claus, you stupid bitch?'

*

I always knew I was different from other little girls. Growing up in a poor area of a huge northern city, you soon realised a lot of people didn't have much. Big families crammed into rows and rows of houses, kids hanging round on street corners near the shops, everyone just getting by. But although money wasn't any tighter for my family than it was for many others, there was something about us which set us apart. When Michael, Simon and I made paper chains out of coloured paper to celebrate Christmas, it was Dad who ripped them down. It was him who made my family different.

While many men in the area went to work as builders or road diggers, Dad didn't. He was a labourer when he met my mum because she babysat for his brother's kids in the evenings to earn a bit extra. She didn't make much at the factory where she was working at the time but even so, the job was a little bit of independence for Mum and earning her own wage meant she had freedom. But it soon disappeared after she met my dad because she gave up her job to marry at twenty-one and have my brother Michael three months later.

My dad, or The Idiot as I like to call him now, didn't seem to see the point of working. He'd given up being a labourer after having an accident and I don't think he ever thought about going back to work and providing for his family because I never saw him lift a finger in his life. In fact, all he did was watch TV lying on a bed he put in the lounge of every single flat or house we lived in. He was too lazy to even sit in a chair and his favourite day was 'pay day' when he collected the benefit money which kept us clothed and fed. One of the only times he got out of bed was to lift weights and build his powerful muscles. Of course, he sat in front of the TV to do it but we all knew how strong he was as he did arm curls or used a chair for squats. His arms and shoulders were the most powerful – big, thick and strong.

But it wasn't the work, or the laziness, or the stains on his teeth which marked Dad out. To the outside world, what set him apart was the fact that he came from a rough family – a big, extended mass of relatives who were like a tribe. His children, though, knew this wasn't the real reason Dad was different. Other people might not have seen it but we knew it was because of a darkness inside him which clung to us like a second skin. At night, we'd dream he was coming to get us and would wake almost too scared to breathe in sheets soaked with urine. By day we were the wildest kids in the area as we tried to forget – climbing on roofs, roaming the streets and getting into fights as kids taunted us.

Dad hated the attention we attracted because it meant the prying eyes of friends, relatives or neighbours were turned on us. So if someone knocked at our door after a fight or a falling out, he'd keep us indoors for days on end to teach us not to make trouble again. The beatings he gave us then were warnings that no one must notice us and he used his hands, a walking stick or a heavy weight-lifting belt to thrash us. I got it sometimes but it was the boys, and Michael in particular, who got the worst.

'Michael, Simon,' he'd scream if he heard them shouting at each other. 'In here.'

Running into the living room, the boys would stand in front of Dad.

'Do you think I can't hear your fucking screaming?' he'd shout. 'Well, if you want to fight so much then get on with it.'

The boys knew what to do without being told. Falling on each other, they'd kick and punch as The Idiot smiled.

Michael always got the better of Simon because he was bigger and my younger brother would end up with a bleeding nose or black eye. But Simon never backed down, and so Michael would eventually stop hitting him because he knew he'd won. Then The Idiot would start on him because somehow Simon never got blamed for the arguments. It was always Michael.

'You're a fucking troublemaker – always fighting with your brother,' The Idiot would shout before slapping or caning Michael.

It's hard to know how often we were hit but there never seemed to be a week when someone wasn't 'getting a doing' as we called it and I knew from the moment I was old enough to recognise danger that there were two fathers inside mine. One had dark brown eyes and a mouth which curved into a smile that could make my heart leap. That was the man who smiled at people in the street and I always hoped I'd be able to make him look just as happy at home. Occasionally I could, like the times he smiled at me when I got into bed next to him to warm up from the freezing cold which made everything in our house feel damp. Or he'd sit up in bed and let me perch on pillows behind him, my legs around either side of his neck, as I searched for pretend nits in his hair.

'A penny for the big ones, a halfpenny for the small,' he'd say with a smile as he leant his head back between my legs.

Those rare times when I made him happy made me desperate to do it again. But as I grew up I learned it was impossible because when the door to the outside world closed, it was as if another man was in our house. If I drew Dad a picture at school, he'd rip it up; if I made him a cup of tea, he'd throw it at me. Then his eyes would turn black, his face twist and his mouth open to scream. We all got burned by scalding tea and food thrown back in our faces.

I lived feeling permanently afraid of what he would do next – always ready to escape if his temper exploded, to run if a slap or object was thrown in my direction. It felt as if a snake was coiled constantly inside the pit of my stomach: sometimes it reared up and bit, but it was the watching and waiting that was the worst.

It wasn't just us kids, though, who were scared because Mum was as well. I knew it hadn't always been like that because Michael told me that when we were little Mum went to the pub with Dad, which meant they must have had fun once. Apparently she was with him there until just a few hours before she gave birth to Laura and back again the night after. The regulars collected £75 for the new baby and marvelled at Mum's fortitude.

But all I can remember is a woman with the same shadow of fear on her face as I felt inside. Just like me, Mum knew that if she got anything wrong she'd be punished. She took it, though, because she knew that if Dad was happy then we wouldn't get a doing.

With beautiful smiling eyes and a plump face, Mum gave me little cuddles when he wasn't watching or washed the cuts on my knee if I fell over. On the nights when he went out to the pub to play darts, she'd put on her Elvis records and sing along as she danced with me. Or she'd rub-a-dub-dub me when there was enough money to warm the hot water for our weekly bath before towelling my hair dry and kissing me goodnight. We all loved her cuddles and kisses and knew Mum did all she could to keep us out of trouble.

'He'll be in here if you don't pipe down,' she'd say as she walked into the bedroom where we were playing. 'Quieten down now or he'll be in.'

If The Idiot carried on ranting, we'd hear her telling him that she was going to deal with us. Then she'd come back to our room and whisper: 'We're going to play a game. I'm going to pretend to smack you and I want you to scream even though it won't hurt.'

I thought games usually made you laugh, like the hide and seek I played with my brothers and Laura. But I'd do as Mum said and yell as loudly as I could because I knew it was better for her that way as well as me. If I didn't play the game with Mum then she'd be punished and I hated it when she was hurt. I didn't see her getting a doing but I heard it happening at night – the shouts and thumps, as if something was being thrown against the wall. The next day Mum would be the one with bruises or a cut lip but she'd never mention it or cry in front of us. I knew what had happened to her, though, and in a way that was the worst thing: seeing the pictures in your mind, knowing it might be you next, but never quite sure when that would be.

CHAPTER TWO

Besides Mum, the person I loved most in the world was my older brother Michael because he was everything I was not. Brave, talkative and full of jokes, I loved him from the moment I can remember. Sometimes we went into the woods to play and sometimes we'd be out on the street but I didn't care as long as I was with Michael. During the day, he'd protect me from the local bullies and at night he'd sneak bread from the kitchen to make us a 'feast'. Sitting on the beds, our stomachs rumbling after a day without food, Michael would break the bread into pieces for Simon, Laura and me. Suddenly a feast would be laid out before us – cream cakes, turkey drummers, jelly and chicken wings dancing before our eyes as Michael told us what each piece of bread had been magically transformed into.

'One day I'm going to run away, find us a pile of money and buy a big house,' he'd say. 'Mum will have her own magic bedroom like a princess and he won't be allowed anywhere near us.'

'I'll stay with Mum when you go,' I'd whisper back. 'And then I'll get a house even bigger than yours and she'll stay with me.'

'No you won't! I'll look after Mum. I'm the oldest so I'll look after her.'

That was Michael's way – he always wanted to protect us. I'll never forget the day I stole a pencil from a girl at school, which Michael in turn took from me because he was my big brother and that's what big brothers did. But later that day the girl's father came to our flat to demand the pencil back. His daughter had told him I'd taken it, his son had seen Michael at school with it, so which of us thieving brats had it? When the front door closed, The Idiot looked at me – his eyes black as the night – and demanded to know what I'd done.

'Nothing,' I pleaded. 'I didn't take anything.'

'Are you sure?'

'Yes, Dad.'

'Well, where's that bastard Michael, then? He got hold of that pencil somehow.'

My brother got a doing that day and I felt tears sliding down the back of my throat when we went to bed later that night because I knew it was my fault he'd been hurt.

'Don't worry, sis,' Michael told me. 'I took the pencil off you so I'm to blame as well and I'd rather be hit by that old bastard than see you get it.'

That was what I loved about Michael. Even though he was just a boy and too small to stop my father's huge fists when they came flying at him, he was the only one who stood up to Dad while the rest of us ran like mice. Michael was the one person in our house who was brave.

No one else really knew what Dad was like. To the rest of the world, he was nice as pie – a bit rough around the edges, maybe, but nothing out of the ordinary. There was just one other person who knew the truth like we did. Mum's mum

Granny Ruby might only have stood about 5ft 2ins but being so tiny didn't make her afraid of Dad.

'Have you no shame to treat your wife and children like dogs?' she'd tell him.

But her visits always ended with Dad yelling at her to get out of his house, so she didn't come too often and after she'd gone, he'd look at Mum and smile at her frightened face.

'Load of fucking nonsense,' he'd say. 'Where the fuck could you go? Who else would put up with a slag like you and your brats? Only me, that's who. I'm the only one stupid enough for it.'

A couple of times I went to visit Granny Ruby's flat nearby and loved it there. It was full of pictures and ornaments and there were also figures of Mary and Jesus on the walls because Granny Ruby was a born-again Christian. Back then, I still believed there was a bearded man in the sky who would protect me even if my dad didn't and so I liked going to Granny Ruby's and seeing pictures of Him on the walls. But my visits were soon stopped. Dad knew I felt safe with Granny Ruby and he didn't want me feeling that way.

The social workers first came to our house when I was about seven. Michael, Simon and I walked in from school to find our parents waiting with a strange man and woman.

'These people have come to see the bruises I've given you,' The Idiot said as he lay in bed.

His eyes were black as he watched us.

'Shut your mouth,' they said.

Fear filled me as I stared at the man and woman. Who were these strangers? People never came into our house. The woman smiled as she walked towards us.

'Someone has told us you've got some bruises,' she said. 'And we've come to see if you're okay.'

None of us spoke for a moment.

'We were fighting,' Michael said in a rush. 'We fell downstairs.'

We knew exactly what we had to say and what would happen to us if we didn't. The lady looked at our faces again before turning to The Idiot.

'Strip down,' he snarled. 'To your underwear. Let's show these people I haven't hurt you.'

I didn't want to take off my clothes but knew I had to. Dad was giving us The Look, daring us to do wrong because then he'd be able to give us a doing when the strangers left.

No one spoke as we stripped until the boys stood in their Y-fronts and me in my knickers and vest.

'Turn around,' Dad snapped.

We stood silently in a row as the strange man and woman looked at us.

'Lift up your vest, Alice.'

I pulled it up to reveal my bare back.

'Now get out and go upstairs,' The Idiot spat.

We grabbed our clothes before running out. Later, we heard the front door slam and I knew the man and woman had gone. We didn't have any bruises that day.

'If anyone asks questions then tell them you've been fighting,' Dad said later. 'I'm going to make sure those bastards don't come back.'

I can remember wondering if I could sneak out of the house and tell the man and woman what Dad did to us all. But I couldn't because then I'd leave Mum, my brothers and sister alone with him and we all needed to stick together.

I don't know who it was who called social services but The Idiot was convinced it was Granny Ruby and screamed at Mum to make sure that 'fucking nosey bitch' never returned. The social services did, though, a couple of times. We never saw them but knew they'd been because they left plastic sheets to put on our beds. They'd seen enough to know our house was filthy — filled with stinking clothes, urine-soaked bed sheets and dirty dishes. It was like a pigsty. You couldn't see the carpet for food and old clothes, mould grew in the kitchen and the flowery cover on the settee was stained brown all over. But that was the way The Idiot liked it.

With bad teeth and the bitter smell of sweat always clinging to him, I never once in my life saw Dad have a bath and he'd spend his last few pence on the gadgets he was obsessed with, like telescopes and binoculars. So although he raked in money from child benefits, there was still often not enough left to buy proper food. He always made sure there was just enough to feed him, though: potatoes and gravy or fried eggs, my mouth would water and my stomach growl when I smelled his food. Sometimes we'd sneak his potato peelings and fry them for our tea but we often went to bed hungry and soon learned to steal food from the local shops or cupboards at home. Of course, we'd get another slap if we were found out but sometimes we were just too hungry to care. Dad would shout, though, if I cried about my stomach gnawing and so I looked forward to going to school because we were given hot food there.

Mum tried to look after us, of course, but it was hard for her because looking after Dad was a full-time job. Making cups of tea, shaving his face as he lay watching TV and fetching and carrying for him, she was at his beck and call and he hated her doing too much for us. She did whatever she could when he wasn't watching too closely; tickling us and making us laugh if she came up to our bedroom, giving us cuddles when his back was turned.

Meanwhile we ran wild: playing hide and seek in the streets when we were allowed out, or in the two bedrooms we all shared on the many days when we were kept inside. There was a third bedroom as well but it couldn't be used because it was piled high with junk The Idiot had collected over the years. So he and Mum slept on a bed in the lounge where he could keep an eye on everyone because that's the way he liked it: nothing could happen in our house without him seeing it or on his say-so. His reeking home was his castle and in it he was king.

Access to the toilet and water was one of The Idiot's favourite ways to control us because he knew he'd be able to endlessly punish us for wrongdoings. We were all so scared that we soaked our mattresses night after night. By the time I was nine, it had got so bad that the wooden bed frames were wet through because there were usually at least two children in each bed at night. With no hot water a lot of the time, the air in our flat was thick with the acrid stink of stale urine.

Once again, Mum tried her best but Dad got so angry if he saw her stripping off the wet sheets that it was easier not to. As I grew older, I also tried to take the soiled bedclothes off the holey mattresses but he'd hear the noises as I moved about.

'What are you up to?' The Idiot would bellow from the lounge and I'd stop what I was doing as I held my breath.

He seemed to love the fact that we couldn't stop ourselves from having accidents at night. Sometimes I'd wake up in time and try to get to the loo. But then I'd hear the creak of his bed as I tiptoed to the bathroom and stop still for fear he'd hear me because he did not like us using the toilet at night. As I stood waiting in the dark for what seemed like for ever, I'd feel a warm stream of urine running down my leg as I wet myself. All of us did it and the carpets were sodden. But The Idiot didn't bother about the stench until he was itching for a fight and then he'd humiliate us.

'Was this you?' he screamed at me one day when he walked into the bedroom I shared with Laura. 'Dirty little bitch.'

He pointed at the sheets hanging off one of the beds. They were stained dirty brown and the springs of the bed were peeking through the ripped mattress underneath. Grabbing me by the back of my neck, Dad started pushing me towards the bed. I knew what was coming and panic rose inside as I was propelled forward.

'Please, Dad, no,' I screamed. 'I didn't mean it. I'll clean it up. Please, no.'

'Shut the fuck up,' he roared as he bent me over the bed.

Pushing my face, he ground it deeper and deeper into the wet sheets. I struggled to breathe as my nose and mouth were pushed into the cold, clammy, stinking bed. The smell was so strong I felt my stomach turn.

It seemed like for ever until my head was finally pulled back and I looked up to see The Idiot standing in front of me.

'Have you learned your lesson now, you dirty little bitch?' he screamed, his hand closing like a vice around my neck. 'Do you want me back in here again?'

I felt so dizzy, my head was twirling as he spoke to me.

'No, Dad,' I whispered.

'Well, then, clean this mess up and if you don't do it properly you'll be sorry, do you hear?'

CHAPTER TWO

He stomped out of the room as I looked around. ᴗ
bedroom windows had been nailed shut after we'd been bur-
gled so there was no way to get fresh air into the place, let
alone dry the washing and air the mattresses. I'd never be
able to do as he said. Fear filled me as I started to cry.

I knew we stunk just as much as our house did so in the
mornings I'd try to wash by topping and tailing myself in
cold water like Mum had shown me. But cold water could-
n't get rid of the sour smell ingrained on my skin and the
other kids at school soon started picking on me.

'Smelly freak, four eyes stinky,' the boys and girls would
cry.

Or sometimes they'd throw bits of paper with messages
on at me in class. 'You stink! Go back to where you came
from.'

I didn't like being alone in the playground, of course, but
it was better than being at home because at least I wasn't
going to get hurt at school. The other kids didn't like me
and called me names but they didn't hit me like Dad did. I
knew I was different because of that but still felt ashamed
when I started getting 'special treatment' because it made
me even more of an outcast. Each day before class I'd be
given a shower and clean clothes to wear by my teacher,
Miss Pritchard, who waited while I washed and helped with
my back if I couldn't reach.

'It'll make it easier for you in class,' she'd say if I started
crying about being different. 'Don't you want to make
friends, Alice?'

I wanted a friend more than anything because all the
other children sat in twos while I was always alone. But I
felt ashamed my teacher was washing me and knew I had to
keep it secret because otherwise I'd be in trouble with The

Idiot. He didn't want anyone helping us. After a few weeks, though, I realised that getting washed might be a good thing because I met a girl called Kirsty who became my first friend.

In the beginning, Kirsty just said 'hi' to me but gradually we started playing together – skipping with ropes, throwing balls, that kind of thing – and soon we were sitting next to each other in class. I was so happy. Kirsty was pretty, wore brightly coloured clothes and her hair was neatly combed into bunches, plaits or ponytails. I wore old sweatshirts and my hair was always straggly because even though I tried to do a neat ponytail, it never looked as nice as Kirsty's.

Just like the showers and clean clothes, I knew I must keep Kirsty a secret from The Idiot because he'd take her from me if he knew. So I didn't whisper a word about my new friend at home and started looking forward to going to school even more. Now I didn't hang around the lunch hall hoping to get a second helping, instead I ran out into the playground with Kirsty. But although I enjoyed having a friend very much, it confused me at times when she told me stories about her mum, dad and the 'family stuff' they did together.

'My daddy took me swimming last night and we played together,' she'd say.

I didn't understand what she meant.

'He put me on his shoulders and threw me into the water. I swallowed some of it but Daddy pulled me up and out.'

At first I told myself that Kirsty must be making up stories because that kind of fun only happened in books. My favourite was the Cat in the Hat who visited a brother and sister and caused all sorts of funny problems. But that wasn't real life and daddies didn't play with you. I only felt safe when mine was out and Laura and I would put on our pyjamas before Mum sneaked us a drink of juice as a treat and cuddled us.

'No carry on tonight,' she'd say as we got into bed. 'Talk quietly and then go to sleep before he comes home.'

But sometimes I'd have bad dreams when my eyes closed and Mum would have to come to see me again.

'Lie back down now and think of something nice,' she'd say and I always thought of cuddling up to her, never Dad. I didn't understand what Kirsty meant when she spoke about hers.

But after a few weeks of being friends, Kirsty told me one day that she couldn't play with me any more.

'Everyone's picking on me too because I'm your friend,' she explained.

'But we can talk when no one's listening,' I pleaded. 'We can be secret friends.'

'No. They'd see us. They'd know.'

And so Kirsty moved seats in class and I was alone again. The only people who never turned against me were my brothers and I knew they were my only real friends as we continued to get up to all sorts of mischief. I think it was a way of releasing all the anger and frustration inside but the adults around us just seemed to get exasperated when we got into yet more trouble. When I was about ten, I was playing tag on a roof with Michael and tried to jump on to a ledge below to get away from him. But I made a mistake and ended up crashing twenty-five feet to the ground below — fracturing both legs, which meant two weeks in hospital and even more time at home with my legs in plaster. Trapped in the house with Dad, I longed to go back to school, though Mum made it better by sitting with me on the sofa or sneaking me an extra bag of crisps. She also tried to make sure I did all the homework sent to me by school but it was hard because Dad had the TV on all the time and, of course, we couldn't turn it off. When I finally got back to school, though, I was as wild as ever with my brothers and no one ever thought to ask why. Maybe they just considered us a bad lot or weren't interested because we were too much trouble, but no one looked closely enough to see what lay hidden behind our front door.

I never knew why The Idiot hated Michael more than the rest of us but it was always him who got it worst because something about him made Dad even more vicious. The slaps were always harder and the words crueller.

'Little bastard,' he'd scream as he whacked Michael with his walking stick. 'You are, aren't you? No son of mine.'

No matter what Michael did, he always got the doing. If Simon hit first, then Michael was the one who was punished for the fight; if all of us got into trouble on the streets, then he was the one The Idiot turned to first with his fists. It upset me to see Michael getting hurt but he laughed it off and would never talk about it with his little sister. We were too young, of course, to find the words but the fact that I was a girl was enough of a reason to hide that he was hurt. When Michael got a second-hand bike, he'd give Simon backies but wouldn't offer me a ride; if we watched a karate film on TV and I tried to copy the moves like my brothers then they'd laugh at me. I was just a girl after all and that was the way things were.

But even though Dad hated Michael more than any of us, there was trouble if someone tried to interfere with his son. I must have been about ten when Michael picked a fight with a boy whose father then came out into the street to finish him off. Michael told us all about it when he got home and The Idiot immediately took out the Samurai swords he kept hidden under the bed and headed out.

'Michael! Get down here and come on,' he shouted as they left the flat.

I don't know what happened when they were out but they hid the swords as soon as they got home. Michael put his under a mattress while Dad stuffed one in the lining of the sofa and we thought that was the end of it. But the police came round later that day and although they didn't find Dad's sword, they easily uncovered the one my brother had hidden. Once the officers had left, Michael got a bad beating from The Idiot for being so stupid and a few weeks later we got home from school to find we were moving.

'This is because of your stupid fucking brother,' Dad said as we stood in front of a Transit van he'd rented. 'I'm going to get locked up because of him.'

You couldn't be sure if it really was Michael's fault, though, because Dad would have blamed him if the moon had fallen out of the sky. Whatever Michael did, he found a reason to use it against him as he screamed and beat him. So I couldn't be sure why we were moving – whether it was the trouble with the police, the visits from social services or something else that had put a new idea in Dad's head – but I wasn't surprised. We'd done it before several times because The Idiot was always falling out with the neighbours and each time we'd load our smelly stuff into a van before moving on to the next home the council had given us.

There was no more talking as we were told to get a move on and pack our things. I only had a few clothes to stuff into a plastic bag but was worried about Laura. She was too small to be packed up and whisked away once again.

'Get in,' Dad screamed, and I knew there was nothing I could do.

I lifted Laura into the back of the van and held on to her as best as I could among all the bits of tired old furniture rattling around with us. No one spoke as The Idiot started driving and I wondered which street we'd be moving to now. But as the minutes slid into hours, I realised we were leaving the city far behind. We were going somewhere new, miles away from anything familiar. I'd always known my dad didn't like prying eyes and now he wanted to get us out from the ever-increasing gaze of first the social workers and then the police. It's true when they say: out of sight, out of mind. We were going to another anonymous, huge city and it would be a long time before the prying eyes found us again.

CHAPTER THREE

We ended up in same city where Tracy, one of dad's sisters, lived with her daughter. Crammed like sardines into her two-bedroom flat, I got my first idea of why Dad seemed to hate Michael even more than the rest of us.

Tracy, who had dyed hair and a craggy face, didn't like Mum. She saw her as an outsider, a steady girl with too much spirit. Later, people would tell me that Mum hadn't taken any rubbish when she was young and when a woman at the factory where she'd worked had bullied her, she'd threatened to cut her hair off with a pair of scissors if she didn't stop.

But by the time we moved, Mum's spirit was beginning to be knocked out of her. She'd try to answer back when Tracy started crowing and cawing after they'd all had a drink together – Tracy liked Black Heart rum while my parents drank vodka and tomato juice. But Dad would always tell Mum to shut up if she tried to defend herself when Tracy went on and on about their brother Pete. He was my uncle whose children Mum had once babysat for and apparently she'd kissed him once before she met Dad. But even years later it didn't take much to set the tinderbox alight.

'I know the way it was,' The Idiot would snap after Tracy had stirred things up. 'You were fucking Pete all the time you were fucking me. That bastard son of yours isn't mine.'

'Of course he is,' Mum would insist. 'Michael's as much yours as the rest of them.'

But Dad wouldn't listen.

'You fucking liar,' he'd shout. 'Making me look after your brats when all the time you were shagging him. You're Pete's ride, Pete's dirty, whorish ride, aren't you?'

However many times Mum tried to tell him – then and in the years to come – The Idiot would never listen and as I lay in the dark, I would picture the smile playing on Tracy's lips as she listened to the fight. I was sure she loved seeing it because she always seemed to be the one who started it.

Things only got worse when we finally left Tracy's for a homeless unit because by then we knew we had to watch ourselves even more carefully than we had before. Staying with Tracy had lent a new edge to Dad's anger and he was even quicker to fly off the handle, even nastier to Mum as he taunted her about Pete. Day after day, he'd berate and belittle her.

'What's this?' he'd scream when she brought him a cup of tea. 'It's too fucking strong, you silly bitch.'

Standing in front of him, Mum would turn away as he screamed, his face becoming red, spit flying from the corners of his mouth.

'But what can I expect from a useless slag like you? You're just Pete's ride, aren't you?'

'No,' Mum would exclaim. 'There was never anything between us but one kiss. I've told you again and again.'

'Fuck off. I know what you are, a dirty whore and it's only me who'd have you. You're a fat bitch and no one else would want you.'

The shouting and bawling seemed to get worse and worse now and I'd lie in bed at night listening to it, feeling sick as I wondered what was happening to Mum. Sometimes she'd appear at breakfast with a split lip or bruises on her arms and, although we didn't see it, I knew Dad was hitting her. By now I was ten, old enough to want to stop him hurting Mum more than anything else in the world and although I knew I was too small to do that, I did the only thing I could – make sure none of us did anything to annoy Dad because it just made him meaner. But soon after moving into the homeless unit Laura and I forgot ourselves because we were just kids after all. I can't remember what we'd done but we got into trouble one day and whatever it was made Dad furious.

'What are you playing at?' he screamed at us as we stood in front of him.

'Nothing, Dad, honest,' I said as I started to cry, hoping that if he saw our tears he wouldn't take the belt to us.

'Haven't I told you enough times?' he roared. 'Don't you know better than to get yourselves into trouble?'

My heart beat as he walked towards Laura and me carrying his walking stick.

'I've had enough of you little bitches,' he yelled as he raised it and started beating our legs.

Laura was only about five, so tiny she staggered as the stick hit her, and I screamed as it smashed into my shins and thighs.

'Get out of my sight,' Dad shouted when he'd finally finished, and we limped out of the room.

Within a few hours my legs felt so sore I could hardly move them. Huge red weals ran livid over my shins and bruises had started to blossom purple under my pale skin.

In fact, the beating was so bad that Mum decided she was going to have to take us to hospital.

'What are you doing that for?' Dad snarled when she told him. 'They're fine. Stop worrying for nothing.'

'Look at them,' Mum insisted. 'They can't go into school like that, can they?'

In the end Dad let us go but lined us up to tell us what to say to the doctors when we got to hospital.

'They'll take you away if you say a word different and you'll never see your mum again,' he told us. 'Just remember that when you're there.'

I felt scared by the time Laura, Mum and I were sitting in casualty. Mum had given our names and we'd been shown to a cubicle before being taken for an X-ray. My legs throbbed as it was done and we sat down to wait again in another cubicle. I stared at the bruises as I wondered when we'd next get a doing. Michael usually got the worst of it but now no one, not even little Laura, was safe.

'There's nothing broken,' the doctor said when he finally came back to see us.

'That's good news,' Mum replied as she started gathering us together.

'But how did this happen?' the doctor asked quietly.

I stared at him.

'We fell downstairs,' I said quickly.

He looked at me, his eyes sliding down to the bruises on my legs before turning to Mum.

'They're always doing it,' she said. 'They play and get themselves into trouble. I was cooking dinner when I heard them tumble.'

The doctor stared at her and I knew he didn't believe our lies. Fear rushed into me. Would he tell anyone? Would

Mum get a beating when we got home? Would someone call the police again?

'Well, you need to take better care of them,' he said as he turned to leave.

Mum looked at Laura and me, legs covered in thick bruises and tears staining our cheeks.

'Let's get you home,' she said.

Relief bubbled up inside me. The doctor wasn't going to get us into trouble, Mum wasn't going to get a beating because we'd been naughty and told Dad's secret. She was safe.

I didn't like the new city where we lived and the kids at school were the same as ever – they just used different names to taunt me.

'Smelly,' they'd snigger. 'Fatty.'

At least the faces in my old class had been familiar ones and I'd known the teachers. This new school was full of strangers and we were even less accepted than we had been before. But I didn't have too much time to dwell on what was happening because by now I had another brother and sister to look after. Baby Kate was about a year old by the time we moved and in 1980 my youngest brother Charlie arrived soon after we left the homeless centre for a three-bedroom house. Now there were six of us: Michael, Simon, Laura, Kate, Charlie and me. I loved Kate from the moment I saw her and felt the same way about Charlie. But Dad didn't seem to like him much because something happened to Mum in hospital when she had Charlie that made him furious.

'Sterilised?' he shouted as they argued. 'That wasn't your fucking decision to make. It's up to me what happens.'

'But the doctors did it,' Mum tried to reason. 'They said

that six children were too much for me. I'm too ill to have more.'

'Well, you should have stopped them,' Dad growled. 'We need more little ones. That's all you're good for.'

I didn't understand why he wanted more children when there were so many of us already. But The Idiot was very angry and Mum had to spend even more time looking after him now to keep him quiet. In fact, by the time we moved into our new house she looked after him pretty much the whole time: if he spat on the floor, she cleaned it up; if he blew his nose and tossed away the tissue, she picked it up. He did things like that all the time and Mum could hardly leave his side without him shouting at her. If she came upstairs to quieten us down, he'd yell; if she left the lounge to go to the kitchen, he'd scream at her to stop.

'Where are you going?'

'To make the kids' tea.'

'Well don't. Get back here. They can look after them-selves.'

'But they're too small.'

'I don't care. Get back here now.'

She had to do what he said otherwise she – or one of us – would be punished and that was why Michael, Simon and I ended up doing so much for our younger brother and sis-ters. The boys helped out with jobs like cooking, which was one of the hardest because we often ran out of gas when there wasn't enough change to feed the slot meter. Sometimes The Idiot sent us out on to the streets to sell some of his precious gadgets to earn a bit of extra money but there were many days when we went hungry. We'd eat cold baked beans and tinned ham if there were tins around or go down to the local supermarket to scour in the bins for food that had been thrown away or wooden crates to burn in the fireplace so we could cook using a big metal pot over the flames. I worried all the time about the little ones getting hurt by the fire but in the end it was me who burned myself quite badly when I sloshed boiling water on my foot one day as I took the kettle off the fire.

The cooking, though, was mostly Michael's job. He was the one in charge of feeding us, Simon helped out with whatever else and I tried to keep our bedrooms and clothes clean and looked after the little ones: doing nappies and bottles, soothing them at night when they lay crying in their cot. Mum was still only allowed to do what she absolutely had to when the babies came along and so a couple of months after Kate and Charlie arrived, their cot was always put in with me and I'd be the one to get up in the night to feed them.

I liked doing it, just as I enjoyed being useful to Mum and the smiles and cuddles my younger brother and sisters gave me. They were still too little to feel constantly afraid like I did and so in between the shouts and beatings, they always seemed to be happy. Of course, they had their tears like all children but I loved looking after them and trying to make our home as nice as possible for them.

Even so, I knew from the time I was a little girl that our house wasn't like other people's. I saw proper homes on the TV – fires in the grate, smoke in the chimney and comfy, clean sofas – but however much I tried to keep things clean, our new house was soon as filthy as anywhere we'd ever lived. Downstairs was a living room where Mum and Dad slept, a kitchen and bathroom, while upstairs there were three bedrooms – one for Michael and Simon, one for the girls, me and Charlie in his cot, and a spare one. There were so many of us that the place was soon a mess: vomit dried hard on baby clothes and stained them, the little ones wiped their bottoms on whatever they could find because we often ran out of toilet roll and one day I opened a cupboard door to find maggots wriggling in excrement buried deep in a pile of old clothes. It wouldn't be the last time. Our new house also got infested with fleas and we were bitten every-where – arms, neck and chest – tiny, itchy bites which ended up getting infected.

I dreamed of a nice clean house like the ones I was sure the other kids at school had but The Idiot didn't seem to notice the filth. In fact, he hated it when Mum and I tried to clean because he'd moan about the smell of bleach and forbid us from using it. All he cared about was keeping an eye on us every minute of the day and we only left the house on his say-so. Occasionally we went out to buy boxes of eggs and sacks of potatoes at a farm, or once every few months we'd drive into the country where Dad took pic-tures of us smiling in the sun like we were a happy family. But mostly we lived in our cramped filthy house or on the street surrounding it and didn't do the stuff other kids did like going to the cinema, for walks or to the playground. We were kept inside because Dad didn't want us making trou-ble. He just couldn't understand that six children were always going to be noisy – even more so if they weren't allowed outside to let off steam – and kept us quiet while he watched the westerns he loved on TV by shouting and bawling or hitting us with his walking stick.

If he did eventually kick us out of the house because we were making too much of a racket, he made Michael keep an eye on us. But my older brother hated having us trailing after him, because, as my eleventh birthday approached, Michael had hit his teens and started becoming a young man. He wasn't a child like us any more – he was getting interested in girls and rebelling. The biggest change in him though was that Michael just didn't seem to care any more if he got hit. Instead, he'd go to his room or leave the house when The Idiot started on him and I wished I was a boy because Michael was brave and being brave meant more freedom.

Beside the dirt and stink, the TV was the only other constant in our home: day or night, it was never switched off. Mostly the screen flickered with cowboy or horror films as my father lay on his bed in front of the TV watching hour after hour of Indian gun fights or masked murderers stabbing knives into screaming women. But as I got older I realised that the films he watched at night often showed pictures of men and women with no clothes on.

Mum tried to shoo us out of the room when those films were on but I saw enough to know I didn't like them. The grunts and shrieks of the people in them sounded painful and sometimes I got scared at night if I woke up needing to go to the loo because I had to walk past the lounge where The Idiot was watching TV. So I'd creep past hoping Dad wouldn't see me, waiting all the time to hear the sheets on his bed rustle, because I knew that if he did catch a glimpse of me then I might get a slap which would send my head spinning.

I was eleven when my body started to mature and Mum told me that soon I'd have to get a bra. I didn't understand what it all meant because I didn't know the facts of life yet but soon after that day, I went in to give Dad a cup of tea as he lay on the bed watching TV.

Just like always, he was wearing a T-shirt because he never really dressed properly when he was at home. But he had managed to shave earlier in the day with a razor, brush and bowl Mum had given him. He said nothing as I bent down to hand him his tea – not too weak, not too strong, two sugars. But as I held out the cup, I felt something on my leg and looked down to see his fingers creeping up my calf like spiders, edging their way up my skin.

I didn't understand. Dad never touched me except to smack me. I stood still as my heart beat. Staring down, I watched his nicotine-stained fingers climb higher. Up and up, underneath my skirt, cold and sweaty, until I felt them pull aside my pants. There was a burning feeling between my legs as his jagged nail scraped me. I did not dare move as he touched me.

'Did you like that?' he asked when he'd finally finished and taken a gulp of his tea.

'What?'

'Did you like how that felt?'

I didn't understand. I didn't want to say the wrong thing and felt sick and afraid as he looked at me and I desperately tried to avoid the sting of his hand on my face or the whack of his walking stick across my legs. Dad said nothing more so I kept silent as his hand moved towards me again, this time creeping underneath the edge of my T-shirt and on to my bare chest. His arms were powerful thanks to the weights he lifted in front of the TV, his skin covered with bristling black hair and his hands rough. Where was Mum? Would she get hurt like me if she came into the room?

'I want to see if you like it or not,' Dad said, his voice husky.

I couldn't speak. I'd seen the films on TV, knew this was something men and women did but I didn't like it. I stood still and silent until it was finally over and Dad picked up his tea once more as a half-smile played across his lips.

'This is our secret, Alice,' he said. 'No one can ever know. I would be very angry if anyone found out. Do you understand?'

His eyes bored into me as he
black as night and I knew what they w
in charge of everything that happened to .
found a new way to control me. We had a secret
keep and if I dared breathe a word about it he'd .
more than he'd ever done before.

CHAPTER FOUR

It was after we moved that The Idiot finally realised Mum wasn't smacking us as hard as he wanted her to. We were still playing the game of yelling loudly whenever he told her to punish us, which happened a lot because you never knew what might annoy him – someone tapping their toe too quickly, one of the little ones crying too loud or the temperature of his tea too low. Without warning, he'd throw his cup and start shouting. Constantly alert, I tried to second guess when he might explode so that I could get Laura, Kate and Charlie out of the way. But sometimes I didn't manage it and a cup would bounce off one of us as we scrambled out of the room.

I'm not sure how he worked out that Mum wasn't belting us hard enough. It was probably because we were usually making a noise again within a few minutes of being punished and he knew how scared and quiet we were after he'd given us a doing. However he found out though, he went wild when he realised Mum wasn't doing as she was told. We were in the living room one day when he told her to smack us and after she had done it his eyes darkened as he stared at her.

'That's not right,' he said quietly.

'What do you mean?' Mum asked as she turned to him.

'You haven't done it properly. Do it again.'

'But I've told them off.'

'Not properly,' he insisted. 'Do it again.'

Mum looked around at us.

'Off to bed now,' she smiled as we looked at her. 'I'll be in soon to say goodnight.'

I could smell anger in the air, knew it was curling all around us even as we started walking towards the door to get away.

'Don't move!' Dad roared. 'You will not leave this room until you've learned your lesson.'

He stared at Mum, his eyes black and dead.

'Deal with it or I will, you dirty bitch.'

Mum was quiet. Ever since Charlie had been born, she'd had trouble getting to the loo in time. Sometimes a stain spread wet across her skirt and it was one more thing The Idiot used to humiliate her. I felt sorry when I heard him taunt her about it because I knew how it felt when he laughed and jeered. Now he stared at Mum, daring her to disobey him. I knew we'd pay for whatever Mum decided: if she didn't hit us again, he'd do it himself far harder than she ever would. But if she did do it, I knew she'd hate herself.

'Do it now, you fucking piece of shit,' he said, his voice low.

She looked at me, unsure for a moment before her hand smacked my legs.

'That's not right,' Dad hissed. 'Do it again and harder this time.'

Mum turned back towards me. There were tears in her eyes as she raised her hand once more. I gasped as she hit me much harder.

'That's better,' I heard him say. 'Now get them out of here.'

From that day on The Idiot watched Mum smack us to make sure she did as she was told. I didn't feel angry with her when she did it. I knew just how Mum felt when she lifted her hand to us. It wasn't just Dad's thick arms or big muscles which made sure he got his own way but the look in his dark eyes as they bored into you. Mum was the same as me. We both had to do as we were told and now that he had started hurting me secretly as well, I felt even sadder about what he did to Mum. Only I understood how terrifying he was.

After the day that Dad started touching me, he did it more and more often. I'd come in from school wearing my uniform – a dark green skirt and sweatshirt – and he'd shout for me to bring him a cup of tea. Panic would fill me when I heard him yell and my heart would beat as I poured the water into the cup I knew I had to take him. When Mum was busy with the little ones and Michael had gone out, I'd go into the living room, every muscle in my body tensed as I waited. After taking the tea, he'd balance it on a tray beside him on the bed before moving his hand towards me. Sometimes I'd stare at the greasy roots of his hair as his fingers crept up my skin or fix my gaze on the filthy carpet as I waited for him to stop, wondering why he was touching me and wishing he wasn't.

'Do you like it?' he'd ask over and over as I stood there shaking, part of me scared of being alone with him and another fearful that one of my brothers and sisters might run into the room.

Sometimes The Idiot would look at me as he touched me, daring me to whisper a word, or he'd ignore me until it was finally over and push me away. Feeling sick and scared, I'd run up to my room and lie on my bed, trying to forget what had happened. But for hours afterwards I could feel him on me, my skin and chest blotchy from where his stubble had scraped me, my breasts sore from being pinched and pulled.

I felt so confused. Was it my fault because I'd started growing up? Had I done something to make Dad do this? I didn't understand why he was so nice in those silent minutes when he called me to him – quiet, his voice soft. Maybe I was a good girl now?

Part of me longed to tell Mum about what was happening but I knew I couldn't. I was eleven years old and felt shame burning inside me even if I didn't understand why. Somehow I knew what Dad was doing to me was terribly wrong and I became even more convinced when I pulled down my knickers one day to find blood staining them. I knew Dad was hurting me and now I was bleeding because of it. But when I told Mum, she just smiled at me.

'You're a woman now,' she said. 'One day you'll have babies, a family of your own.'

I looked at her, dreaming of the day when I would be away from Dad, and Mum could come to live with me just as Michael and I had always promised. I couldn't wait for that day. She and I would be safe, Michael would be happy and the little ones would be with us too. But I should have known by now that my dreams would never come true and it was after my periods started that Dad found a whole new way to torture me. It was a couple of weeks later when I arrived back from school to hear him shout for me and my heart hammered as I walked into the living room, knowing what was waiting.

'Get yourself changed,' Dad snapped.

My chest felt fluttery as I ran to my bedroom before going back downstairs. The Idiot stared at the skirt I was wearing with a T-shirt.

'Have you got your pants on?' he hissed and I turned to run out of the room.

I knew he was annoyed with me. I'd been stupid again. He did not like me to wear underwear. I must do as he said.

As I ran upstairs, I heard the front door slam and the house go quiet. Walking back into the living room, I looked at Dad.

'Where is everyone?' I asked.

'I sent them out so we could have some time alone together,' he said as he fixed his eyes on me. 'They've gone to the shop. Now lock the front door.'

My heart thumped as I walked out of the living room. I had never been alone in the house with him before. What would he do to me this time? How long would it be before Mum got home? Turning the key in the front door, I felt a soft click as the lock slid into place. I was alone now, trapped on the inside with Dad. I pushed down tears as I walked back to where he was waiting.

'Lie down,' he said as I walked to the edge of the bed.

My stomach twisted. He'd never asked me to get on to the bed with him before. Heaving himself on to his feet, I saw he was wearing one of Mum's long T-shirt night-dresses – it was white with a picture of a teddy bear on the front.

'Lift up your skirt,' Dad said as I lay down and he crawled on to the bed beside me.

He threw himself on top of me, his weight crushing the breath out of my body, spit clinging in strands at the side of his lips. His hands gripped my arms as he moved on top of me. He stank of smoke. I couldn't breathe. He was killing me. I could feel his hands clawing at me, his huge belly crushing the air out of me as pain exploded inside.

'Do you like it?' he panted.

I did not make a sound as he carried on hurting me.

'Do you like it?' he said more roughly and I knew what I had to tell him.

'Yes,' I whispered.

Afterwards I lay on my bed, my knees drawn tight up to my chest, as I waited for the pain to ease. I stayed hidden upstairs when I heard Mum and the kids come home and fill the house with noise just like always. I felt so scared because I was sure Mum would know what had happened when she saw me. It would be written on my face just as her fear was. But I could not hide any more when I was shouted downstairs for tea and knew I had to go.

'You look pale,' Mum said as I got my food.

I stared at her – a part of me almost hoping that somehow she'd see my secret and rescue me from it; that she'd know what was happening without words just as I knew what was happening to her even if I didn't always see the bruises. But Mum didn't seem to notice as she carried on serving out the watery sausage stew she'd made for that night's tea.

I took my food and went to sit down on the living room floor where we always ate. Looking around, I stared at my brothers and sisters. Little Kate, who was two, six-year-old Laura and baby Charlie. Then there was Simon and finally Michael, my brave older brother whom I knew would never let such a thing happen to him.

'Do you want yours, Alice, or shall you give it to me?' he asked as he smiled at me.

'You have it,' I said, and pushed my plate towards him.

'Michael!' Mum said with a laugh. 'You shouldn't be taking Alice's food like that.'

Michael laughed as he piled his fork and shovelled a piece of sausage into his mouth. I stared down at my hands as they twisted in front of me. Ever since Dad had started touching me, I'd kept asking myself one question: what had I done to deserve it? Now I knew the answer. I must be what Dad had told me I was – a good-for-nothing little bitch – if the people I loved most in the world couldn't see the pain carved inside me. I deserved what was happening. Just as he kept telling me I did. It was our secret and no one must ever know how bad I was.

CHAPTER FIVE

Maybe it made sense to The Idiot's twisted logic, but I didn't understand why he slapped me less often after he started abusing me. The others soon noticed and teased me for being his favourite. It felt as if they were backing away from me, or maybe I was backing away from them, but whatever it was it made me feel lonely. I would far rather have got the slaps and beltings than what happened to me when Mum and the kids were sent to the shop.

Locking the door just as Dad told me to, I'd try to escape as he heaved himself on to me by imagining I was somewhere else – a beach, far, far away, a warm and quiet place where no one could hurt me. Cutting myself off from the stink of his skin, I'd wait until he'd taken what he wanted before pulling down my skirt and leaving the room.

A few times he gave me money afterwards.

'What's this for?' I asked.

'You,' he replied. 'But don't tell anyone about it.'

Once, Mum asked him where a five-pound note was that I knew was hidden in my pocket because he'd just given it to me.

'Don't know, don't care, just get out of my fucking face,' he hissed.

Mum didn't say anything as she left the room.

'Do you want it back?' I asked The Idiot, feeling my fingers wrap around the note.

I didn't want an argument or for Mum to get hit for asking too many questions because of me.

'No I don't. Just get out.'

I used the money to buy sweets for the younger ones but as they pleaded for more, I felt something inside me snap. They were so tiny and clingy, I could never do enough for them. I just wanted to be on my own, lying on my bed, hiding from the noise, cries and laughing. I spent more and more time alone now in my room, shutting Laura, Kate and Charlie out and telling them to look after themselves. I hated myself for being unkind but was sure that somehow I'd made Dad do what he'd done to me so I had to keep away from them because I didn't want the kids being hurt like me. But each time I tried to clear my mind when I finally lay down on my bed, all I could hear were Dad's words ringing round my head.

'You can never tell anyone about this, you know.'

'I'd make sure you paid if you told.'

'No one would believe your lies.'

It usually took about twenty minutes for Mum and the kids to get back from fetching bread or milk at the shop. But no matter how much I tried to blank out what was happening when they were away, it was always real. Sometimes I'd pray Mum would hurry home but she never could because the little ones were with her and they walked so slowly. I was left alone with Dad until it was finally over, he told me to unlock the door and I let the world back into our house.

The Idiot mostly hit us on the body where the bruises didn't show but as I got older I saw the marks he sometimes left on Mum. I must have been about eight when I first noticed her lip bleeding and from then on I'd see it was cut every now and again, a trickle of blood running from her nose or finger marks on her wrists.

'Pete's ride, dirty slag,' I'd hear him screaming.

'I'm not,' she'd cry.

'You are, you stupid bitch. You can't do anything. You can't even cook, can you? You're fucking useless.'

There were times, of course, when he left his marks on us – like the day we were all carrying on upstairs and he shouted up for us to quiet down because he couldn't hear the TV. But the kids were too small to take much notice and soon we heard him climbing the stairs.

'What did I tell you?' The Idiot roared as he walked into the bedroom where Laura, Kate and I were hiding under the bedclothes.

I wrapped my arms around them as we lay in the semi-darkness. I could hear him shuffling towards us and the sound of his belt slicing the air as he lifted it.

'I've told you all again and again,' he screamed as the weight-lifting belt crashed down on us. 'Shut the fuck up when I'm watching TV.'

The belt came crashing down – feet, head, face, it didn't matter which part of us it hit and I pulled Kate to me. She was only tiny and I could hear Charlie screaming in his cot.

'And you can shut that little bastard up too,' Dad screeched when he'd finally finished, his breath coming in gulps after giving us a doing.

There was never a question in my mind that Dad would carry out his threats if he really wanted to. He had knives and swords hidden under the bed and kept a lump hammer and tomahawk near him all the time. There was also a stiletto knife with a long diamond-shaped blade that he had under his pillow in case anyone attacked him. I don't know where he got the idea from that he might one day be the one who got beaten, but he seemed to be permanently preparing for it. His fascination with weapons only grew stronger as I got older and he built up a knife collection which he constantly cleaned. As well as a Rambo knife with a huge blade and a compass at the top of the shaft, there were throwing stars and knuckledusters. He also had two dozen throwing knives which he kept wrapped in cloths and hidden in a locked metal box. After oiling them, he'd practise throwing a dozen, one after the other, at an old door he used as a target. Sitting on the bed, he'd fling the knives across the room as we stood by.

'Pick 'em up,' he'd yell when he finished, and we'd scurry to collect them.

Sometimes when he was angry he'd hold the knives up as he looked at us.

'You'd better buck up your ideas because you're not going to get away with your cheek,' he'd hiss, and my stomach would swoop as I looked at the long, sharp knife in his hand.

I think that's why secrets were never spoken of in our house. For so long after Dad started hurting me, I longed for Mum to stop him. But it felt as if whatever happened, she'd never realise what he was up to. One day she got back from the shop with the kids to find the door still locked. The Idiot had taken longer than usual and I hadn't had a chance to open it yet.

'Why's the door locked?' Mum asked when I finally turned the key.

'He told me to do it,' I said as I turned away from her, not wanting to look her in the eyes.

Mum didn't say anything as she carried the shopping in with the kids following her. They were dragging after her – Kate whining, Charlie crying, Laura lagging behind – as she walked towards the living room.

'Can you change his nappy?' she asked as she handed Charlie to me. 'He's wet through and I need to get your Dad's tea on.'

Nothing more was said as I took my brother and started walking upstairs. I understood why Mum did not see what was happening: she was too scared to.

By the time I was twelve, Michael had grown up. Even though he was just a couple of years older than me, he looked so big now and, almost as tall as Dad, he refused more and more to play by The Idiot's rules.

'Where have you been?' Dad would scream when my brother walked in late from school. 'You're supposed to walk your brothers and sisters home.'

'I got a detention,' Michael would shout back. 'And anyway, I'm not their bloody chaperone.'

Black anger pooled in The Idiot's eyes as he swung his walking stick and my brother dodged out of his way.

'Get back here, you little bastard.'

But Michael would run upstairs or out of the house as we scurried away.

'Leave him,' Mum would sometimes softly urge.

'Shut up,' Dad would yell. 'He's under my roof and I will not have that little bastard disobeying me.'

But nothing he said or did seemed to frighten Michael any more and it made Dad really angry. He was used to getting what he wanted because we were so young and easily scared. But Michael had used Dad's weights to build up his muscles, and getting stronger physically seemed to make him braver. My brother refused more and more often to do as he was ordered. Sometimes he didn't come home at night or would disappear for hours in the day and The Idiot's rage would fill the house.

'Get upstairs, all of you,' I heard Dad screaming one day when I was in the kitchen.

Michael had just come home and I ran into the hall to find The Idiot pinning him to the wall by his throat.

'No, Dad,' I screamed. 'Leave him.'

But The Idiot wouldn't listen and he clamped his arm tighter across Michael.

'I said get upstairs now or does one of you want it too?' The Idiot roared.

I grabbed the little ones and we hid in a bedroom. Downstairs I could hear shouts until the house eventually quieted down and Michael came upstairs. There was a red mark on his face and his eyes were blazing.

'One day I'll kill him and then I'll run away,' he spat.

I think that was the reason why I never dared tell Michael about what was happening to me, because I was sure he might try to carry out his threat if I did and then he'd be the one killed. As my brother became more and more rebellious, I could feel The Idiot's anger spinning out of control: he was the one in charge, the one who threw things, slapped or whipped to keep us in line. But nothing he did now made Michael afraid of him. The battle raged until one night Michael stayed out again and Dad called the police to bring him home. The Idiot did that whenever he felt like it: rang the police to make trouble for someone he'd fallen out with. I'd been out to the shops when I walked in the door to find my brother lying half on, half off the stairs with The Idiot standing over him.

'Do you think you can do what you like in my house?' he screamed. 'Do you think you can use this place like a fucking hostel?'

The veins on his neck bulged as he spat at Michael lying beneath him.

'You are going to do as you're told, you little piece of shit,' he screamed.

Michael's eyes blazed as he struggled to get up.

'I will not,' he shouted. 'I won't hear a word you say, you evil old bastard.'

'Aaaah,' Dad roared as he lunged towards Michael with a broom.

Grunting with the effort, he started beating him with it.

'Stop it,' Mum screamed. 'Leave him alone.'

But Dad wouldn't listen. Again and again, he smacked the wood against Michael, swearing as he did so. The kids cowered behind me as my brother was beaten. Dad wasn't going to stop. He would kill Michael this time, make sure he could never defy him again. I knew I had to get the kids away. Grabbing them, I pushed them up the stairs. But as we ran into the bedroom, I heard a loud crack as the brush handle broke across Michael's back.

'Get off me, you old bastard,' my brother yelled as he screamed in pain, and there were bangs and thuds as they fought.

Seconds later I heard the front door slam and ran to the window. Michael was running down the path as Dad stood at the door screaming at him.

'Don't ever come back, you little bastard. This is my fucking house and I will not have you in it.'

I wondered if that was really it this time but was pretty sure it wasn't. Where else would Michael go? And how could he leave us? He had always promised that one day he'd take all of us away and he wouldn't leave without us. The house was quiet for the rest of the day and no one mentioned Michael. But the next day when I walked into the kitchen with Mum to make a cup of tea, I noticed her hands were shaking as she lifted up the kettle.

'What's wrong?' I asked as she turned on the tap.

'He's not coming back,' Mum said softly.

'Who?'

'Michael.'

I stared at her. That could not be true. Michael would never leave us. He always came back in the end.

'What do you mean? He'll be back.'

'No, he won't,' Mum said as she turned towards me.

There were tears in her eyes.

'He won't be coming home. He's going to live with Granny Ruby.'

'But that's miles away! How will we see him?'

'We won't.'

'What do you mean, won't?'

'I mean he's gone, Alice, and he's not coming back. You've seen what it's like. Your father and Michael just can't see eye to eye. It is better for all of us if he isn't here.'

My heart hammered in my ears. I couldn't believe what Mum was saying. Michael could not have gone. He was the one who stood up to Dad, he was the one who would save us all one day when he ran away and we went to live in the big house he'd get for us.

'But he can't be gone,' I whispered as I stared at Mum.

She didn't look at me as she bent her head.

'He is, love. He won't be coming back now.'

I was alone.

CHAPTER SIX

Kate's nickname was Kitty Kat. Small and skinny, she started topping and tailing herself from the age of five because she was so independent. She also learned how to plait hair and loved playing with mine at night as we sat in our bedroom. Laura had a fiery temper and a softer side in turns, while Charlie would cry for hour after hour when he was a teething baby and I'd have to take him out in his pram so that he wouldn't disturb The Idiot. By the age of three, he still wouldn't be without a bottle and Dad would smash them against the wall because he didn't want him having them any more. But Charlie would scream so much without it that eventually Simon would have to go down to the shop late in the evening to buy him another.

Simon was only a year younger than me so I didn't look after him much and he spent hours alone in his room dismantling old electrical gadgets, like a top-loading video recorder, before putting them back together again. Meanwhile I was usually so tired after running around with the kids that all I wanted was to sleep at the end of a day. Even that was hard, though, because while Laura and Kate were supposed to share the queen-sized bed in our room while I had a single, we'd all end up together in the big bed when they got scared and I'd cuddle them as the shouts downstairs rattled through the floor.

When he got older, Charlie would also crawl in with us and I'd spend the night getting up to put him back into his bed before feeling him sneak back in soon after. I didn't have the heart to keep moving him but always made sure he was back in his own bed by morning because The Idiot hated him being in with me.

I looked after the kids even more after Michael went. Mum was busy as usual looking after The Idiot and I found that if I kept running after the little ones until I finally fell into bed then I wouldn't think too much about Michael. I missed him so much even though I knew he'd done what he had to. Looking after the children helped me forget the ache in my stomach for him and also made me feel close to Mum because I knew she missed Michael as well. Dad wouldn't hear his name spoken and occasionally when the phone went, she'd whisper quietly into the receiver until The Idiot realised who it was and told her to hang up.

'You'll have nothing to do with him,' he'd scream. 'He's gone and that's it. You'll be sorry if I catch you talking to him again.'

Mum never argued back and I understood why she didn't as I got older and began to see the thousand different ways he controlled and humiliated her – like making her sit on the end of his bed for hour after hour, ready to be at his beck and call whenever he needed her, or making her wait for an hour when she asked for a cigarette before throwing it at her, or telling her to shut up until he allowed her to speak. He was like a puppet master who pulled her strings whenever he felt like being cruel and I never heard a kind word come out of his mouth. It was always 'fat bitch' this or 'stupid cow' that and Mum's strength to stand up to it slowly drained away as her health got worse. By now, as well as the bladder problems she'd developed after having all of us, her chest was bad and she took pills for a thyroid complaint.

Because Mum was weak and ill, I tried to do as much as I could for her – looking after her almost like I looked after the kids. There were moments when we were alone together and I made her happy as we smiled about one of the kids' latest jokes or bought pound presents for Christmases and birthdays. Then we were just like any other mother and daughter and I knew I would do anything to protect her. But at night I would silently cry as I heard muffled screams. Mum never spoke about it but I knew she and I were the same: Dad hurt her hidden behind closed doors just like me. Sometimes I'd ask her how she'd got the bruises and she'd tell me she'd banged into a door, or I'd find her crying in the kitchen.

'Are you okay?' I asked as she wiped her eyes.

'I'm fine, darling,' she'd tell me as she tried to smile.

'Are you sure?'

'Yes, of course. I'm just a bit tired. I need a good night's sleep and I'll be fine. Now why don't you help me get the tea on?'

But then came a day when Dad lost control and I saw for the first time just how vicious he was on all those nights when I heard the shouting. It was after Michael had left home and a phone call came to say he was leaving Granny Ruby's to go and stay with one of The Idiot's sisters. He went wild.

'She's not going to take him in,' he yelled. 'He's not going anywhere near my family. He can look after himself.'

'At least we'll know where he is,' Mum said quietly.

'I don't give a fuck where he is and neither should you. I don't want to hear any more about him.'

'But I want to know he's safe.'

Dad lurched towards Mum as he roared: 'How dare you? That bastard is dead to us.'

Raising his hand, he slapped her across the face before punching her in the stomach. I stared in horror as Mum's breath was knocked out and she stumbled back. I wanted to run to her, stop him from hurting her but suddenly Dad turned around and yelled at me to get out. The look in his eyes told me I had to do as he said.

Panic filled me as I lay on my bed listening to the shouts and it seemed like for ever until she finally climbed the stairs. Mum looked as if she'd been crying as she walked into my room and there was a red mark on her face where she'd been slapped.

I started sobbing as she sat down beside me.

'What are we going to do?' I whispered.

She pushed my hair out of my face and patted my hand.

'Stay out of his way,' she replied.

Her voice was flat. No sing-song in it, no laughter, no warmth. Just lifeless.

'But can't we go and find Michael? Live with him?'

'He's just a boy, love. He can't help us.'

'There must be somewhere we can go. Anywhere. Just get away.'

Mum looked at me quietly.

'Where? We've got nothing or no one. He's made sure of that.'

I don't know if it was because Michael had left or whether my new school had contacted them, but soon the social workers came back into our lives again. Once again, I was spotted as the needy one in class and given clean clothes to wear. Of course, the teachers soon realised what my dad was like and I had to hand the clothes back in at the end of each day, otherwise he'd swipe them. There were only so many times I could lie that they had been lost and I'd bring them back on a tomorrow which never came. Dad was so mean, he'd take anything he could get for free and I even had to start hiding from my cookery teacher because week after week I'd take home food that he'd eat before refusing to pay the 50p we were asked to give for the ingredients.

Just as I had been when I was younger, I was an outsider with few friends – the only ones I really made were twin sisters called Lucy and Sarah. Lucy had been badly burned in a fire when she was young and got picked on just like me so we stuck together. She didn't mind the way I was and I didn't mind the way she was. I knew her scars were on the outside while mine were hidden. Lucy had to have skin grafts to try to repair her scars, which she said were very painful as she described the treatments she had at hospital.

'So why do you do it?' I asked one day.

'Because I have to if I want a normal body and a normal life,' she replied, and I wished there was a treatment that could make me whole again.

Maths and reading were the subjects I liked best but I didn't really try in classes like geography because after a lifetime of being told how useless I was, I knew I was too stupid to understand them. There were some subjects I didn't even get a chance to do, though, like gym or swimming because The Idiot didn't want me wearing a short skirt or a swimming costume.

'Stay away from those idiot boys at school,' he'd tell me when we were alone together. 'Because if I ever catch you with one of them then I'll make you pay.'

Mum tried to tell him that I had to do sport but he refused to listen. I never learned to swim or ride a bike and took notes into school excusing me from gym. In fact, I didn't do any of the things the other girls in my class did but no one seemed to really notice. Sometimes I thought someone would, an adult would see how withdrawn and uncommunicative I was and want to find out why. But there was just one teacher who once asked me if I had any problems at home. I didn't really know her very well so I told her I was fine because in a way it was true. At least when I was at school, I wasn't at home with him and I could dream in peace of being a nurse or an air hostess, who flew off to the places I read about in books. But the moment school ended, I knew I was his again as the chains he was slowly wrapping around me clamped tighter and I ran home.

At the end of each day I'd leave lessons five minutes early, run down the corridor to the changing room and rip off the clothes I'd been lent that morning so I could leave school the moment the bell went. Then I'd rush home without stopping to chat to Lucy because otherwise The Idiot would ask questions about why I was late. The leash he kept me on was tightening all the time and after Michael went, I was told to stay in the house more and more. Where I'd once been allowed out, I was now told to keep in; if I was sent to the shop, I had to come straight back; if I tried to go out and play with the little ones, I'd be told to get inside. My father was starting to build a prison around me but I had no idea what he was doing as the bars enclosed me. I was just a child and woke up with just one thought each morning: that he would not call me to see him today and force me down on to the bed again.

No one else noticed what he was doing – not even the social worker who visited one afternoon when I'd just got back from school. The woman who knocked on our door looked like an old hag with a severe face and grey hair and I could see she was dying to get out of our house almost as soon as she stepped into it. After looking at the toilet, which was filthy with mess that had built up because we weren't allowed to flush it at night, she opened the doors to our bedrooms to find wet mattresses and excrement-stained clothes. The stench of urine washed over her and, holding a hand in front of her mouth and nose, the woman blinked her eyes rapidly as the bitter smell burned into them.

'You're going to have to help your mother,' she said as she looked down at me. 'She can't do it all.'

The social worker must have stayed all of fifteen minutes before she left and Dad was furious we'd been found again. He was told the house needed cleaning up and so he went out to buy pine disinfectant and Brillo pads, which Mum and I used to scrub the bad bits off the carpets. We pulled mouldy clothes out of cupboards, threw old newspapers away and collected up all the dirty nappies I'd tried to keep in a bin but which had been scattered around. We cleaned up food trodden into the carpet, tossed stained clothes into bin bags and picked up ripped underwear off the floor. When it was finally done, The Idiot came to inspect our work and opened cupboard doors and drawers to see if it was all to his liking. To be honest, I didn't know how to clean a house properly because I'd never lived in something that a normal person would consider habitable, so I hadn't done a good job and neither had Mum. But Dad's standards were so low that he'd have thought a pigsty was a palace and he seemed pleased.

'Just make sure it stays this way,' he said. 'I don't want those social work bastards back in this house again.'

It was always the same: The Idiot did everything he

could to stop anyone entering the world he had created for us and we moved on whenever there was too bad a fight with a neighbour. No one ever knew us well enough to look too closely at what was happening behind our front door and I was like every other abused child – believing I must deserve it if something terrible was happening to me week in and week out and no one noticed the pain I was in.

Charlie was four and I was fourteen when I got called out from class one day and told I had to go and pick him up. I'd dropped him off as usual at nursery earlier that day so I wondered what had happened as I walked to get him. When I got there I was told Charlie had bitten a little Indian girl so badly his teeth had sunk through her tights and into her skin.

'You're going to have to ask your parents to come and see me about this,' the head of the nursery told me. 'I really don't think we can cope with Charlie any more. He's so disruptive, so unruly and this really is the last straw.'

I knew Charlie was wild. Even at such a young age, he swore and cursed because he'd heard The Idiot do it so much. After a lifetime of seeing horror films on the TV and watching the real-life slaps, he used to hit me without reason and lash out when he lost his temper. But at other times, he acted like the little boy he still was and cuddled up to Mum and me until Dad told us to put him down.

'Do you want to make him soft?' he'd snarl.

I wondered what would happen to Charlie now. Mum wouldn't be able to look after him properly at home so he'd be left to fend for himself until he was old enough to go to school like us older kids.

The Idiot was annoyed, of course, when I told him what had happened. Charlie getting expelled was another bit of trouble for him so he made sure my little brother got a good smack to know he wasn't pleased. But in the next breath, he started laughing as he looked at him.

'That's my boy,' he crowed. 'You got the Paki bastard good and proper.'

Charlie looked up at him, not knowing if he'd done good or bad. He was too young to understand that my father was so racist he refused to even step into the local shop because it was run by an Indian family. He said anyone with a skin darker than his was a robbing bastard and would always park outside while I ran in to get what he wanted.

But even though The Idiot enjoyed Charlie's attack on the little girl, he soon realised his expulsion was going to cause a problem. No other nursery would take him and Dad's solution was simple: I'd have to stop going to school so much and look after my youngest brother. It was the perfect excuse for him to keep me away from the one place where he knew I might make friends and find a way to break his spell over me. School was the only escape I had and now he could stop me from going because if anyone asked, all he had to say was that I was needed at home. My mum was sick and I had a baby brother to look after.

From then on I was kept indoors nearly all the time – only occasionally allowed out to see a neighbour, Mrs Smith, whose daughter was in a wheelchair, or attend the odd bit of school. If I was kept off in the morning, I'd sometimes go in for the afternoon, or if I had a PE lesson after lunch I'd go home early. The teachers gave me homework which I knew would never be looked at because I'd be too busy watching Charlie. The only time I wasn't in charge of him was when Dad sent him and Mum to the shop to get something and I had to stay indoors so The Idiot could take what he wanted. What had happened every couple of weeks now occurred at least once a week after I was at home more with Charlie. I never fought against Dad or screamed when he wanted sex but to me it felt as if I was being raped again and again.

I just wanted to be like other girls my own age – learning at school and spending time with friends. But I knew I was not like my classmates and slowly I began to accept that I never would be. I stopped even dreaming of a normal life. Dad made sure I'd never have one every time he touched me. I was just a girl but he made me feel used and dirty, like an old rag no one wanted, as he slowly shut off the outside world from our home. Once Mrs Smith might have been invited in to have a drink at Christmas but now she was not allowed past the front door. The only time I really got to see normal life was when I was sent to the shop with a note listing what we needed but even then it was just a quick dash down the road and back again.

Mum couldn't write very well so I'd do the list for her each time: bread, milk, a packet of Woodbines for her and small cigars for him. Sometimes she'd ask me to sneak a quarter of chocolate raisins on to the list and I'd write down half a pound to make sure we all got a taste.

So I'd run down the shop with the note and the man there would send me back with what we owed written down on a piece of paper. That way Dad never saw the chocolate raisins on the list and didn't realise we were getting them. After running into the house with a bag of shopping, I'd sneak them to Mum in the kitchen and she'd hide them in a cupboard or the washing machine. Later, when gun shots and cowboy screams, or the moans of naked men and women, blared out from the TV Dad was glued to, she'd slip some of the sweets into my hand.

'Go and give some to Laura, Kate and Charlie,' she'd say. 'And make sure Simon gets a couple too.'

Folding my hand gently around the chocolate raisins, I'd walk back into the lounge. Dad had blocked off a door to the kitchen to make sure no one could get in or out without walking past his bed in the living room because he wanted to know every detail of what we ate and drank. Stuffing my hand into my pocket, I'd walk slowly past before running upstairs and he never noticed that I was carrying treasure.

It felt so good to do one tiny thing Dad did not know about but he must have sensed my defiance like a dog sniffing out a bone because soon he started timing my visits to the shop.

'What took you so long?' he'd snarl when I arrived home.

'Nothing,' I'd reply.

'Well, what were you up to?'

'I just went there and back.'

'No, you didn't.'

'I did.'

'You fucking didn't. You were gone twenty-five minutes and it doesn't take that long. Who were you talking to? Were you chatting with those boys you're at school with?'

'No. I didn't speak to anyone.'

'You'd better not be because you're for it if I catch you. I've told you to keep away from boys, do you hear?'

'Yes, Dad.'

'So what were you doing?'

'Nothing, I promise.'

'Well, next time you're late you'll get a hiding.'

After that I knew he was watching the clock on the wall each time I left for the shop. I had fifteen minutes walking time plus five to buy what was on the list otherwise there'd be trouble. But even though I always made it home on time, he soon found another reason to be vicious.

'Where's my change?' he asked one day as I walked into the living room.

I'd run home because there had been a queue in the shop and my heart thumped as I stood in front of his bed. He was lying in a vest as he barked questions at me.

'Here,' I said as I walked up and dropped the coins into his hand.

'There's a pound missing,' he said softly.

'There can't be.'

'There fucking is. Where is it?'

'I don't know.'

He stared at me silently, his eyes darkening.

'It must have dropped out of my pocket,' I said in a rush. His lip curled up.

'You lying bitch. You've spent it, haven't you?'

The Idiot got up out of bed and leaned towards me. Pushing his face into mine, he breathed in deeply as his nose almost touched my mouth. I felt sick as I smelled the stench of him so near me.

'Did you buy sweets?' he said softly.

I could hear him breathing in, smelling my breath to see if there was a clue hidden in it.

'No, Dad. I didn't, honest. The money must have dropped out of my pocket.'

He stepped back and looked at me.

'Well then, turn out your pockets if you've nothing to hide.'

I pulled at the greying pockets of the jacket I was wearing. There was nothing in them.

'Take off your shoes and socks,' he said as he stared at me.

Once again, there was nothing hidden away that I didn't want him to see. I wouldn't have dared do such a thing. But still Dad wasn't content because if there was one more way to torture me he would find it.

'Well, you'd better get back outside with your brothers and find my money,' he hissed as he sat back down.

I felt sick as I looked at him. I'd never find the money on the street now. The kids round here would have had it as soon as it fell out of my pocket. But I knew I'd have to do as he said and spent ages with my brothers searching, all the time feeling more and more afraid of what was waiting for me when I got home empty-handed.

'Don't you ever lose my money again,' Dad shouted as he slapped me until my head span. 'Now get out of my sight.'

Turning around, I ran out of the room. If I'd ever dared hope I might save some of his money and use it to run away, I knew I'd never be able to hide so much as a penny from him now.

Sometimes Dad used protection when he forced himself on to me, but by the time I was thirteen he decided he wanted me to go on the pill. I stopped taking it just before my fifteenth birthday because it gave me awful headaches. But even though I'd learned more about the facts of life at school by now, no one had ever mentioned what was happening to me. When it first started, I'd wondered if other little girls secretly did the same thing with their dads. Now I knew they didn't and for that reason alone was sure I could never get pregnant because a daughter couldn't give birth to her father's child.

Deep down, though, I was still scared. But even in my darkest dreams – the ones in which I saw Dad's face coming towards me and felt his breath on my skin before he pinned me to the bed – I could never have imagined what he wanted from me. My fear, though, didn't disappear just because I refused to feel it and soon my periods stopped for months on end. The doctors ran tests to find out why but told me there was no physical reason so it must be because of stress.

I think now that my body was trying to stop me from giving The Idiot what I was terrified he wanted but I did not realise it then. All I knew was that there was nothing I could do to stop him having sex with me whenever he felt like it. If I was upstairs and the house went suddenly quiet, or if I was seeing to Charlie and heard Mum calling the kids to put on their coats because it was time to go out, I knew what was going to happen even before he shouted for me. As sure as waves crash on to a beach and the sun rises and shines, this was the pattern of my life now.

CHAPTER SEVEN

The ground swallowed me up in blackness as I fell towards it.

'Alice?' a voice enquired, and I opened my eyes to see Mum holding a wet cloth above me.

'What happened?' I asked.

I felt sick and dizzy as I looked up.

'You've fainted,' she said as she put the cloth to my forehead. 'Lie still a minute and then we'll get you up. I think you knocked yourself on the fireplace when you took a fall.'

My head hurt as I sat up and looked around the room. I didn't know what had happened. One minute I was fine and the next I'd blacked out.

'What's the fucking problem now?' Dad snarled from his bed.

'She's fainted but I'm going to take her up to the hospital because she hit her head.'

'Well, be quick about it because I'll be wanting my tea soon,' he grunted.

Mum took me up to the hospital and we waited while the doctors did some tests to find out what was wrong.

'Have you been eating right?' Mum asked as we sat side

by side. 'Maybe that's why you're poorly. You're off your food sometimes these days.'

'I'm fine,' I insisted.

We sat and waited until the doctor came back to talk to us.

'Is there anything you want to tell your mum?' he said as he looked at me sternly.

I felt suddenly afraid.

'It's time to tell your mum the truth,' he said again, his voice hard.

My head rushed. Did he know about Dad? Could he tell from looking at me? Shame rushed up hot inside me as Mum turned to me. I knew I could never tell her about what had happened. It would hurt her more than she could bear. She was not strong enough.

'Alice?' Mum asked.

Silently, I stared at the doctor.

'She's pregnant,' he snapped.

The ground fell from beneath me. My head felt light. It couldn't be true. It couldn't be happening. I could not have a baby. His baby. It wasn't possible.

'No,' I whispered as a rush of sickness burned the back of my throat.

I wanted to run out of the room, away from these eyes staring at me and searching for the secrets I knew I would never share.

'Well, you are and I'm sure you know how it happened even if you are only fifteen.'

The doctor's voice sounded rough and accusing, his eyes bored into me as I sat statue still, my head rushing and my heart pounding. I couldn't speak as questions were fired at me.

'When was your last period? Have you had any morning sickness?'

I stared at him.

'But I haven't done anything.'

My words only seemed to make him angrier.

'Well, of course you have.'

Mum looked at me.

'What's this, Alice? Whose is it?'

'A boy at school,' I whispered.

Mum started pulling on her coat as she stood up.

'I think we'd better get home,' she said, before thanking the doctor and leading me outside.

'Oh, Alice,' she said as she looked at me. 'What are we going to tell your dad? You said you'd wait. You promised me you wouldn't get into trouble. What's he going to do when he hears about this?'

I didn't know what to say, how to explain this thing growing inside me. I was too young to have a baby. I could not let the proof of what a terrible girl I was grow inside.

When we got home, The Idiot started raging the moment Mum told him the news.

'How the fuck did this happen?' he screamed. 'What have you been up to, you little slut?'

But even as he shouted, I could see a smirk playing at the corners of his mouth. I didn't understand. He was happy. He thought this was funny.

'What did the doctor say?' he snarled when he'd finally quietened down and Mum had left the room.

'Just what Mum told you. I'm pregnant.'

'No. About the father?'

'Nothing. I didn't tell him anything.'

Dad looked at me as I stood at the edge of the room.

'What am I going to do?' I whispered.

He walked towards me and stood close.

'It's all right,' he replied softly.

I looked at him confused. How could it ever be all right? I was carrying his child. My father's baby.

My mind rushed as I wondered what he meant before I suddenly realised. I'd heard about terminations, knew you could get one if you didn't want a baby. Was he going to help me?

'Your mum and I will look after you,' Dad said, and my throat tightened as he stared at me. 'We'll help you. We'll work it through.'

I looked at him, my mind edging towards what I knew he meant until coldness spread through my body.

'I can't have it,' I whispered. 'You know I can't.'

He stared at me, a smile still almost playing at the side of his lips as his eyes narrowed.

'Of course you can,' he said. 'And you will.'

I could not think or feel when I realised what Dad was going to make me do. I had to close myself off like a tap or else I would be overwhelmed with the horror of what was happening to me. It was not a baby inside, just a thing and I wanted it out of me more than I'd ever wanted anything before. I'd have done whatever The Idiot asked of me just to get rid of it. Revulsion filled me if my mind even flickered towards thinking about my pregnancy and I'd imagine pushing something sharp inside me or throwing myself out of a window to kill what was growing within me and myself too. At night I'd pray as I lay in bed and listened to the sounds of the children breathing around me. Maybe if I asked Him enough times then He would make sure the baby was not born. It could not be born.

But how could I stop it? Dad kept an even closer eye on me now – he watched me all the time as he told me to drink more water because I had terrible morning sickness and he thought it would make it better. I knew nothing would make it better when I crouched over to be sick. It wasn't what was inside me that was making me ill. It was my feelings pouring out. I felt trapped like a caged animal as Dad waited and watched to get what he wanted. I felt so alone. I knew Mum was angry with me even though she didn't shout and scream. Instead, she kept asking questions I couldn't answer.

'How could you have been so stupid, Alice? Are you still seeing him? What's this boy's name? He needs to know what's happening because he's as much responsible as you are.'

I told her many times it was an older boy who'd left school so I didn't know where he was. But Mum wouldn't stop asking questions until The Idiot finally told her to leave me alone.

'Will you shut up?' he yelled one day. 'Just leave her alone. There's nothing to be done. We've just got to get on with it.'

I supposed he wanted me to feel grateful he was protecting me. He'd even stopped wanting to have sex or hitting me since he found out I was pregnant but it made me feel even more afraid because he seemed so happy. I'd never felt anything like it before; my heart would hammer inside me when I thought about what was going to happen and I wanted to tear at my stomach to stop whatever was growing inside me. I was so afraid that Mum would find out that I'd betrayed her by letting Dad touch me or that the police would discover I had done something so wrong. But most of all I was afraid that my baby might actually be born.

'Another little one,' The Idiot would say as he looked at me from his bed. 'How are you feeling today?'

I couldn't tell him because I didn't know. It was as if I were

watching a film of someone else's life or having a nightmare
I could not wake up from. Was I really so bad that something
this terrible could happen to me? I hated what was inside me
so much that I wanted to die.

There were moments when I thought about telling
someone. But who would possibly believe what my own
father was doing to me? He'd always told me I'd get in
trouble if I told so what would happen to me now I was
having his baby? I also thought about running away. But
where would I go? And what would happen to the kids if I
went? I couldn't take them with me because there were too
many of us and I couldn't leave them – or Mum – alone
with him.

So my life carried on as normal: I got my brothers and
sisters up out of bed and did them a breakfast of bread
and margarine before taking them to school. Some days I
then went into school myself but on others I walked home
after dropping off the kids and spent the rest of the day
in the house before going to pick them up again. Each
day dragged by and I felt more of a prisoner than ever
before; I was trapped by the baby as well as Dad and all I
could do was hope that I'd lose it. I waited several weeks
before I woke up one morning to find I was bleeding.

'It happens sometimes when a woman is carrying,' Dad
said. 'I'm sure it's nothing to worry about.'

But when Mum took me to the accident and emergency,
I was told the baby had gone. Relief crept around the edges
of my numbness as I went home and Mum told The Idiot
what had happened.

'What did you fucking do?' he later hissed.

'Nothing. I just woke up and I was bleeding. The doctor
said there was nothing I could have done.'

'Well, you must have done something. Did you jump

around too much or have too hot a bath? What have you been up to?'

'Nothing. I've done nothing.'

'You're telling me that you didn't want this to happen?'

'No, Dad. Of course not.'

'So that means you're just fucking stupid then. So useless you can't even carry a baby. You're good for nothing, aren't you? Just a fat, stupid lump.'

I didn't speak as I turned to walk away. I felt confused by how nasty he was being when he'd been so nice before. Dad was right. I'd wished this baby dead and I was glad it was gone.

Reaching out to open the door, I felt a hand on my arm.

'Don't worry,' Dad said softly. 'Maybe you're too young now and your body's not ready.'

I looked at him, wondering if his kind words would come with a kick or a slap. I knew he was angry with me and he wouldn't let it go this easily.

'We'll leave it a year or so,' he said as he drew near.

'What do you mean?' I asked dully.

'Just what I said,' he whispered. 'We'll leave it a year and then we'll try again.'

My heart went cold as I heard those words. This was not an accident that would never happen again because Dad would be more careful. He had wanted this baby and he'd stop at nothing to get another one.

CHAPTER EIGHT

A few weeks after the miscarriage, I left school just before my sixteenth birthday without taking any exams. I'd liked to have stayed on but knew I wouldn't pass any exams even if I took them because I'd missed so much school. Besides, Mum needed help at home and Dad had told me I had to start signing on so he could get some extra money. I was as trapped as I ever had been as my world closed down to the four walls my father ruled. I wanted to die, to let the blackness which filled me drown me for ever. Soon after the miscarriage, I gulped down a handful of painkillers I'd been prescribed for migraines but woke up feeling drowsy hours later.

I wouldn't get my wish and knew I had to carry on because the little ones needed me. What would they do if I was gone? I might not protect them from Dad's belt and stick but I dried their tears when he hurt them, whispered comforting words when they were scared and held them in the night. Mum and I were all they had and she needed me almost as much as they did. But the despair I felt had to be released somehow and I started cutting my arms and legs with razors because as the blood ran out of my skin I felt the pain leave me for a moment. I couldn't stop thinking about the baby. What had I done to make my own father do that to me?

I lived more and more in the shadows and The Idiot's desire to control me only got stronger. I wasn't allowed to go shopping for my own clothes – instead he picked them for me and I wore the same shapeless leggings, skirts and jogging bottoms as Mum. Later my hair was cut and permed in the same style as hers so that we looked very similar. I was not even allowed to choose what underwear to wear and was never measured for a bra or given any clothes which clung a little tightly or dipped too low on my chest.

Slowly my father was moulding me just as he had done Mum: making me so terrified that he could do whatever he wanted with me. Sometimes I tried to refuse what he wanted by pretending that I had my period because I knew then he wouldn't touch me. But I could never keep away from him for too long because he just got meaner when he wasn't getting what he wanted. If I refused him, he just got more violent towards Mum and the kids because he knew the best way to control me was to hurt the people I loved.

'What's this shit?' he'd scream at Mum when she gave him his dinner.

'This tea's too cold,' he'd yell before throwing the cup at her.

Without words, he told me that if I kept myself from him then everyone else would suffer and it made me feel so guilty. No matter how much the children cried or begged, The Idiot still did whatever he wanted to them and I would only make it worse by angering him. So in the end it was easier to give in when he dug his fingers into my arm and pulled my face close to his.

'You're to do as you're fucking told,' he'd snap. 'Now get your underwear off and get washed.'

I didn't have a choice if I didn't want anyone else getting hurt so I'd go to him in the living room after he'd sent Mum and the little ones out to the shops. I felt dead inside as I lay on the dirty bed while he humiliated me and I stared at the wallpaper pattern – a big leaf with a brown centre and small green leaves around it. Over and over, I'd draw pictures in my mind, tracing the edges of the pattern, my eyes going round and round the lines until I reached the bottom of the wall and raised my eyes to start again. I just wanted to be apart from myself until it was over and after the baby died I learned how to switch myself off inside. It was like turning off a light – everything went dark until he told me to get out of the room and I knew it was over. A few months after the miscarriage, I had to go back to the doctor because I was sleepwalking at night – shouting and moaning as I got out of my bed and wandered around my prison. He gave me drugs to calm me down but didn't ask why a sixteen-year-old would be so anxious – just as the teachers or social workers had never really seemed to want to know. I felt invisible both because I was hidden away by my father and because no one else seemed to want to see me when I was let out.

Nothing got in the way of Dad's plans: when Simon left school the year after me, he made sure my brother got a paper round so he was also out for a few hours each day. Trapped at home looking after the kids, I started claiming benefits when Dad ordered me to apply for them. Each week I'd collect my money and he'd take every penny from me to spend on himself. Everything I had was his and when the kids were at school, Mum had been sent to the shops and Simon was out, he'd force me to give him sex.

Sometimes I wondered if he'd get bored with torturing me one day and decide that he'd had his fun. But that day never came and I could see in his eyes that it never would. I felt that I was just what he told me: worthless, good for nothing, bad through and through, because who else was this happening to? I had seen normal girls at school and was certain they did not suffer as I did so I also knew that I must have done something to deserve it.

Sometimes Mum would arrive home to find the door still locked if I was still with Dad but neither of us spoke a word about it when I eventually turned the key and walked back into the house. If the kids were with her, they'd moan about being stuck outside but no one said anything about the locked door. I think it was almost accepted because everyone had got so used to it. Alice stayed at home with Dad while the kids went with Mum to the shops.

Looking back, I know now that people don't ask questions they don't want answers to and I think Mum was like that. I kept telling myself she couldn't know what was happening because it hurt too much to think that she might. But after the miscarriage something happened that really confused me and for the first time I wondered if she did actually know. It was one afternoon as I was just pulling down my T-shirt because The Idiot had finished pawing me and Mum walked into the room.

'What's going on?' she asked.

'Nothing,' I said as I ran out. 'Nothing's going on.'

Mum did not come after me but that night I heard shouts and knew her questions were being silenced by Dad's fists. She never mentioned that day again and it convinced me even more that everything must be my fault because if Mum would not talk to me about it then surely I had done something wrong? I'd always felt guilty about what was happening – as if I was betraying her by letting Dad do what he wanted with me – and the suspicion that she knew just added to the million different voices rushing round inside my head.

There were moments, of course, when I felt anger flicker up and wondered why Mum didn't speak out. I wanted her to stop Dad and protect me. But I pushed my feelings down because I knew she was as scared as I was. A lifetime of curses and insults, slaps and whippings, had made her as much of a prisoner as me. Mum didn't want to acknowledge what she couldn't bear to face and by speaking out she'd have made it real, so she kept silent.

But it was real to me and I dreamed of killing Dad over and over again. At night I'd see his face leering towards me, during the day my head ached with migraines as I tried to stop myself thinking. I clung to one dream: that some day Mum would find the courage to run away with me and the kids. I don't know why I thought that might happen. I should have known even then that Mum was like me – too scared to go against Dad because she knew that what-ever she did, he would dream up a punishment far worse than she could ever imagine.

The Idiot made sure we knew that by constantly remind-ing us what he was capable of – like the day he and Mum went shopping and arrived home to find a crossbow bolt had been fired into the video cabinet. Simon had been mess-ing around with the weapon and accidentally set it off. But although Dad had always encouraged his interest by taking him into the garden with an air rifle and showing him how to shoot or letting him throw knives at trees when we occa-sionally went into the country, he was furious when he got home to find someone had touched one of his precious weapons without permission.

'Who was it?' Dad demanded as we all stood in the living room. 'Which one of you fired it?'

'Leave them,' Mum pleaded. 'I'll deal with it.'

'No, you fucking won't.'

The Idiot was holding a stiletto knife as he stared at us, twirling it as he screamed. My stomach turned as I stared at it. I was sure he'd use it if we made a wrong move and I didn't want the little ones getting hurt. Rather me than them.

Walking down the line of children, Dad questioned each one of us.

'Was it you?' he shouted at Simon.

'No, Dad, honest.'

'Was it you?' he screamed at me.

My heart beat as I stared at the knife. I knew that he could stab me with it in an instant if he wanted to.

'Simon done it, Simon done it,' one of the little ones yelped in fright.

Turning around, Dad grabbed a hammer and we scattered as he threw it. We managed to get away without being hurt but Simon got a bad smacking that day and never dared touch anything of Dad's again. None of us forgot how close we'd come to having that knife in our guts.

Another day, I heard a fight starting as Dad rounded on Mum and I ran to the living room with the little ones following behind. Flinging open the door, I saw Mum pinned to the wall.

'Pete's ride,' The Idiot screamed. 'You're just a useless piece of shit, aren't you? Don't you dare answer me back.'

Fear filled me as I saw a knife in his hand.

'Dad, no,' I screamed. 'Leave her alone. Let her be.'

'Get the fuck out if you know what's good for you,' Dad roared as he turned towards me.

I looked at the knife again. I felt sick inside, shaky as I looked at the blade. Would he use it this time?

Mum was still as she stood pushed against the wall but I knew what I had to do when her eyes slid towards me. Closing the door, I grabbed the kids' hands and ran upstairs. It was just as it had always been: Mum would take the beating whenever she could just to make sure we didn't get hurt and the reason I didn't help her that day was the same as she had for not helping me – it was better that one person got hurt than all of us.

'You know that no one will ever want you?' The Idiot whispered in my ear. 'There will never be a man who looks at you.'

I hung my head as he spoke to me.

'Now do it,' Dad snapped, and I felt his hand on the back of my neck, forcing my head down.

He hadn't made me do this before and I didn't want to. At least I could turn my head away and switch myself off when he forced himself inside me. All I had to do was lie there and pretend I was dead. But this was different and I didn't want to go near him or do anything to him.

Trying to push my head back up, I felt his hands force me back down again. He had pulled up the T-shirt he was wearing and was naked from the waist down.

'Stop your fucking wriggling, you useless cow,' Dad snarled.

He pushed himself into my mouth and the bitter smell of urine washed over me. It was so thick and strong that it felt like it was filling me. I retched as The Idiot pulled my head up and down. Gasping for breath, I felt sick as the smell of him choked me. He smelled like an animal in a cage – bitter, acrid and unclean. But he wouldn't let me go. Again and again, he pushed my mouth up and down. I couldn't breathe or move as the stench of him filled my lungs.

'Use your fucking tongue,' he shouted. 'You're not doing it right. Suck it, do it properly.'

It seemed to go on for ever until at last I heard The Idiot groan and felt his hands slacken. I couldn't bear it, I couldn't do it again. I felt sick. The smell of him. The dirt on his skin. His hands pushing at me.

As I raised my head, I felt the back of my throat watering and knew what was going to happen. I tried swallowing it down but it was too late. Vomit poured out of me – splashing The Idiot and falling on to the floor beside the bed.

'What the fuck are you doing?' he screamed.

I felt his hand slap me around the back of the head.

'Dirty bitch,' he roared. 'You did that on purpose, didn't you?'

'I'm sorry, Dad,' I said as I tried to scrape the mess off him. 'I'm so sorry.'

I didn't want him to punch me or worse. I could see his knife box under the bed next to me.

'Get a fucking cloth,' he roared.

'I'm sorry. I didn't mean it. I won't do it again.'

'No, you fucking won't, or you know what will happen, don't you? Just get me cleaned up and get out of my sight.'

I ran into the kitchen, put a tea towel under the tap and went back into the living room.

'I'm sorry,' I kept repeating as I tried to clean him.

'You're worse than useless, aren't you?' Dad snapped. 'You can't do a thing right, you useless slag. If you do that again I'll kick your cunt in.'

My head felt light and I wanted to be sick again but I kept swallowing it down as I scrubbed at Dad's lap. Why couldn't I get rid of the mess I'd made? I had to clean off the stain or he would go for me. I thought of the weapons lying close – the sharp knives, the throwing stars with their sharp points. I had to do whatever he wanted or he'd kill me.

'Hurry up!' he yelled and I scrubbed even harder.

Suddenly he bent his head down towards mine and looked at me.

'You really are a stupid bitch, aren't you? You need to practise that and get better.'

Kneeling on the floor, I looked up at him.

'Because it's all you're good for, isn't it? Cleaning up, looking after the kids and lying on your back.'

'Yes, Dad.'

'Are you listening to me, you dumb bitch?' he screamed as he raised his hand and I flinched. 'Don't go getting ideas about a boyfriend or nothing. I know what you're up to when you go to the shops. I know you're eyeing up the boys and hoping one of them might give it to you. But who would? Who would ever think you could be anything other than a used piece of skirt? You're damaged, used goods, fit for nothing and you'd be in just as much trouble as me if anyone ever found out what we did. They put slags like you in prison, you know.'

I pushed back the tears burning the back of my throat.

'Can't do a thing right, can you?' he sneered as I got up to leave.

'No, Dad,' I whispered.

All the time, The Idiot was watching and waiting to get what he wanted from me. It only took a few months for my periods to stop again and when they did I knew I'd been forgotten by the god I'd prayed to. After a week of waiting, I told Dad and he smiled as he heard the news.

'When were you due?' he asked.

'Last week.'

'So why didn't you tell me before?'

'Because I thought it would come.'

'Well, get down to the chemist and get a test done. Here's the money.'

I felt a scream ripping up inside me as I walked into the pharmacy, wrote my name on a slip of paper and gave in a urine sample. The minutes slid by until a lady walked up to me and handed me back the slip of paper I'd written on. I unfolded it and saw two words on the page: positive and negative. The box beside positive was ticked. The ground swooped beneath me as I walked home to tell Dad.

'Good,' he said with a smile, and turned back to the TV.

Of course, I had to tell Mum as well and the words felt thick in my mouth as I formed them, the lies suffocating me as I spoke.

'It was a one night stand,' I said. 'A tumble in a bush with a local boy on the way home from the shops. I couldn't help it. I'm sorry.'

She didn't speak and for a moment I wanted Mum to start firing questions at me – so many that I'd have to break down and tell her the truth of what was happening. She didn't say anything to me but later I heard her go into the living room to tell Dad what he already knew.

'How did this happen?' she asked.

'How the fuck do I know? Your daughter's a slag just like you.'

As the weeks slid by, I silently prayed for the baby to bleed away inside me just like the last one. I pictured it just as I had before – blood pouring out of my body as it left me. I felt terrified every minute of the day. Maybe this time I would have to have it but I knew I could never love it. I would hate it almost as much as I hated myself for letting this happen. I knew you were supposed to feel happy if you were pregnant and my feelings were just another sign of how rotten I was. It wasn't the baby's fault yet still I hated it.

I grew more and more afraid as the weeks passed: eight, nine, ten . . . the baby was inside me. Eleven, twelve, thirteen . . . it still wouldn't let go. Sometimes I woke up in the night and felt tears on my cheeks. But as the weeks passed, I shut myself down inside again and refused to let myself think about it. I felt so ashamed and dirty and knew that if anyone ever found out the truth, I would be punished. Dad had always told me that. If only I had been born a boy, he wouldn't hurt me like he did.

Finally my prayers were answered when I started bleeding two days after Christmas 1986 and knew my wish had been granted. I was taken to hospital for an operation and felt free as I woke up and knew it was over. But as soon as I got home, I felt despair wash over me. My first pregnancy had been over so quickly, I'd been almost able to pretend it hadn't happened. But this one had gone on long enough to plant roots of terror deep inside. Why couldn't anyone see what was happening?

'You need to be more careful, Alice,' Mum told me one day as I lay on my bed. 'You're only sixteen – too young for all this. You need to wait and find the right person to settle down with. Will you think about that for me, please? I want you to be happy in the future with a husband and children but now is not the right time. You have your whole life ahead of you.'

How did she not know it was being stolen from me every day? I didn't want to live any more and withdrew into myself, hoping that I would somehow die.

'You're a useless bitch,' The Idiot told me later. 'What did you do to the baby? Did you want this to happen?'

It was a question without an answer. It didn't matter what I wanted. I was just a thing – a body he beat when his fury was ignited or abused when his desire peaked. I knew it was only a matter of time before he made me pregnant again. I was a prisoner and my father was not going to release me until I had given him what he wanted.

CHAPTER NINE

Kate curled her hand around my swollen stomach.

'What do you think it is, Alice?' she asked. 'A boy or a girl?'

'I don't know. Now stop talking otherwise you'll miss the next bit.'

It was April 1988 and I was nearly eighteen. Pregnant for the third time, my baby was due in the summer. But as Kate turned her head towards the TV screen and cuddled into me, I could almost feel happy for a moment: curled up on the bed with the kids and able to forget as we lost ourselves in a film. *Bambi* and *Lady and the Tramp* were my favourites while Kate and Laura loved *Chitty Chitty Bang Bang*.

Once more I'd frozen myself up inside when I realised I was pregnant again and I tried to stop myself having the baby by throwing myself out of bed and taking more of the pain relief pills the doctor had given me than I was supposed to. But the baby had stayed inside me and I didn't want to think about it now as I pulled my sister closer to me and stared at the screen. I'd told Mum the father was a friend of Michael's who I'd known since I was young and had bumped into again at the shops. This time she didn't ask questions about how I'd managed to have sex with a boy when I was only allowed out for a few minutes at a time.

'Make sure nothing happens to this one,' Dad had told me when we got the news.

Of course, I hoped it would and twelve weeks had passed while I prayed for the bleeding to start again. But it hadn't and fear filled me when I realised there was no escape. I hated the baby growing inside me even more than The Idiot's smile when he stared at my expanding tummy. Sometimes he made me stand in front of him naked so he could look at me. It was as if I was precious now I was giving him what he wanted.

'Make sure you save some milk for me when the baby's born,' he'd say with a smile.

He sickened me but in spite of myself I knew there was another emotion waiting to be felt inside. It had bubbled up out of me one afternoon when I was upset by another of The Idiot's spiteful outbursts that I should have been so used to. It happened when I walked out of the kitchen squabbling with the kids.

'Will you lot shut up?' he screamed as he picked up the hammer he kept by the side of his bed and flung it.

I felt a thud on the edge of my stomach and white-hot fury filled me.

'What the fuck do you think you're doing?' I screamed.

Dad's eyes hardened as I shouted at him and I suddenly remembered who I was talking to before walking away. But later I felt confused that something had made me protect my baby even for a moment. I'd wished it dead from the moment I knew I was having it. I didn't want this child any more than the others, couldn't imagine how I could ever survive having The Idiot's baby. I didn't want to think about it as the weeks turned into months and my stomach grew and grew. Sometimes Mum would talk about how things would be after the baby was born but I'd turn away. I wouldn't talk about it or feel anything for something I hated.

Turning towards the TV, I shifted my weight as I tried to concentrate on the film. I couldn't stop thinking about my brother Simon. Earlier that day, I'd gone out to help him on his paper round because I wanted to get some fresh air. I'd been stuck inside so long because I was hardly allowed to leave the house now but Dad sometimes let me out if Simon was there to keep an eye on me. On the way home though, I'd got a stitch and the pain had cut through my side as I puffed and panted. Simon had told me to sit down long enough to get my breath back and rubbed my stomach until I felt well enough to walk home. We'd arrived ten minutes late and Dad had grabbed me as soon as I got through the door.

'Where have you been?' he yelled as he started shaking me by the shoulders.

'I didn't feel well. We had to stop.'

The Idiot whirled around to look at my brother.

'What the fuck are you two up to?'

I didn't understand why he was so angry. He'd let me go out with Simon before, he knew we wouldn't do anything to disobey him.

'What are you talking about?' I pleaded. 'I had a stitch. Simon helped me.'

Dad's eyes darkened even more.

'I bet he did. What the fuck has it got to do with him?'

'I had a stitch,' I shouted. 'He rubbed it better.'

The Idiot drew closer to me, his eyes flashing.

'He did what?'

'He rubbed my stomach to make the pain go away.'

Dad pushed me by the shoulders and I stumbled back as he started screaming.

'Is this baby his, then? Is that what this is all about? Are you fucking him?'

'No,' I screamed as fear made my heart beat.

'What are you talking about?' Simon yelled. 'What are you saying?'

I looked at him, pleading with him silently to let me calm Dad back down.

'Simon just helped me, that's all,' I said.

'So what were you up to?' The Idiot snarled.

'We had to stop until I felt better. That's why we were late. There's nothing else to it.'

But The Idiot would not listen. Suddenly he spun around to face Simon as the veins in his neck bulged and I knew nothing I could say would calm him down now.

'Do you think I don't know what's going on?' he screamed. 'Do you think I don't know what you two are up to?'

'Nothing, Dad,' Simon insisted. 'Nothing at all.'

'You're a fucking liar,' Dad roared as he hurled himself past me at my brother – his hands clenched into fists. 'Is this little one yours? Have you been messing with your sister? I'm going to fucking kill you.'

Simon darted away as my father lurched towards him.

'Leave me alone,' he screamed. 'Get away from me.'

The Idiot threw himself towards Simon as my brother's hand closed around the door handle.

'Come back here,' Dad roared.

Wrenching open the door, Simon ran outside as The Idiot tried to grab him.

'I've had enough,' my brother screamed. 'Do you hear me? You're fucking mad.'

'Come back here, you little bastard,' Dad yelled. 'Get back here right now.'

'No. I've had enough, do you hear? I'm sixteen now. You can't tell me what to do. You can't beat me when you feel like it any more. I'm going to get you charged, see if I don't.'

The Idiot stopped at the door as Simon ran off. He was panting as he stared after him.

'He'll be back,' he hissed. 'Now get inside and close the door. We don't want the neighbours poking their fucking noses in.'

The house had gone quiet as we did what Dad told us but Simon had not come home since the row and now I wondered where he'd gone as I sat with the kids in front of the TV. Would he do as he'd promised? Surely he wouldn't dare?

'Can I get a drink?' Kate asked, and her voice pulled me back to the present.

'No,' I said. 'You stay here and I'll get one for you.'

Walking out of the bedroom, I started going downstairs. It was quiet in the living room. In fact, the whole house was quiet. Like the silent moments before a storm begins.

The police arrived a few hours later to tell Dad that Simon had made a complaint about him which they were now investigating.

'He's out of control,' The Idiot told them. 'This is ridiculous. He's just a troublemaker.'

But the officers just listened silently before telling Dad they'd be back. It was clear they were taking whatever Simon had said seriously and, when the door finally closed, The Idiot started ranting and raving.

'That little bastard brother of yours,' he screamed. 'What the fuck does he think he's playing at? He's told them I attacked him and now they say they're looking into it. I'll fucking kill him.'

I couldn't believe it. No one had ever gone against Dad like this before. There was no knowing what he might do now. I couldn't believe Simon had actually done it. Didn't he know what would happen to us all?

Dad took a deep breath as he walked towards me, his eyes fixed on my face.

'You're to keep your mouth shut, do you hear me?' he spat at me. 'If you so much as breathe a word of what went on then you'll be sorry, do you hear? Don't say a thing about what happened today. They can't do anything as long as it's our word against his.'

I nodded slowly, knowing I wouldn't dare speak out, whatever Simon had said. All we could do was wait now to see what might happen and for the next couple of days, Dad let me take the kids to and from school but apart from that no one was allowed out. He seemed fidgety, almost scared, as he sat and watched TV, waiting to see what the police would do. He'd hidden us from prying eyes for so long and now they were trained on us again. We'd run from the social workers and police before but this time it felt different and The Idiot was furious because there was nothing he could do. If there was one thing in his miserable life he'd always had power over it was his kids – he'd been able to scare us into obeying him for years and years. But first Michael and now Simon had stood up to him. I knew that if he ever got his hands on Simon then he'd beat the living daylights out of him.

We crept around him, keeping out of his way, anxious not to give him any reason to start on us, as he brooded on what had happened. It was like being in a war and waiting for the enemy to attack. I felt restless because I was sure that if our secrets were told then Dad's revenge would be worse than anything we'd seen before. Going in to see him in the living room, I would stare at the knife box under the bed or think of the nunchucks — two thick sticks connected with a chain — hidden away or the crossbow in its box. After trying to protect us all for so long, would it be impossible to stop Dad carrying out his threats now one of us had turned against him? I kept thinking about what Simon had done, wondering how he'd dared do it and praying it would not get taken too far because otherwise there was no knowing what might happen to us all.

Nothing happened until a couple of days later when I walked Laura, Kate and Charlie to school and noticed a car parked outside that I was sure I'd seen near our house when we left. I looked inside to see a man and a woman watching us.

'I think someone was following us when I took the little ones to school,' I told The Idiot when I got home.

I wanted to be sure he didn't have a reason to start on any of us.

'What do you mean?'

'There was a man and a woman in a car. It was parked here when we left and then again at the school.'

'Who the fuck are they?' Dad hissed as he got up and walked to the window.

He pulled the curtains shut and shadows fell across the room as the TV flickered in the corner.

'Don't answer the door,' he snapped.

We spent the day at home as usual — Dad peering outside every now and again, Mum and I silent. She had been even quieter than usual since Simon had gone. She was like an animal that has dug itself into its shelter and is waiting for the danger to pass. But as I was getting ready to go and pick up the kids later that day, the phone rang and she answered it.

'Hello?' Mum said.

She didn't speak for a few seconds but I watched as she listened to the person on the other end and her face drained of colour.

'What do you mean?' Mum said. 'Who's got them?'

I stood, unsure of whether to leave the house or not, as Dad grabbed the phone from her hand.

'What's this?' he spat. 'What's going on?'

He was silent for a moment before screaming again.

'Listen to me, you fucking bitch. I'm coming down now to pick up my little ones. You can't keep them.'

He slammed down the phone and started yelling.

'That bastard Simon. The kids have been taken into care. They got them at school. Social services have them.'

I didn't understand. All I knew about social services was that they'd turned up their nose at the smell in our house and left some plastic sheets to put on the beds years before. How could they have the little ones now? This was their home. I was on my way to pick them up and bring them back.

'What do you mean?' I asked uncertainly, looking from Mum to Dad and then back again.

'They've been taken from us, you stupid bitch,' The Idiot spat. 'We're not getting them back until those bastards have snooped around.'

I felt a rush of panic inside. The little ones couldn't be gone. They were all Mum and I had. They were what I held on to, the one thing that gave me a reason to keep breathing.

Mum walked out the room as Dad grabbed hold of me.

'You're not to say a word about anything,' he hissed. 'Do you hear me?'

'I won't, Dad. I promise.'

He drew close.

'I mean it. I'll kill you if you open your mouth.'

His eyes were black as the night.

'Do you understand what I mean? If they come for me then I'll make sure I cut you and your mum into a thousand little pieces before they take me away. Bit by bit, piece by piece, I'll kill you both. Do you hear?'

I didn't say a word.

'Do you hear me, you little bitch?' he snarled as he pushed his face towards mine.

'Yes, Dad.'

I knew he meant what he said. I, of all people, understood what he was capable of. The baby I was carrying was proof of that.

CHAPTER TEN

A knock sounded on the door about half an hour later and Dad opened it.

'What's this all about?' he snarled.

Standing on the doorstep were two officers.

'We need you to come with us, sir,' a man said. 'Allegations have been made by your son and we need to talk to you.'

'Simon's a liar. This is slander. He can't get away with this.'

Dad was put into a waiting car and as the door closed he glanced at Mum and me to remind me of the threat he'd made. Fear filled me as I stared out of the window watching the police car drive away. What would he do to us when he got home? A man and a woman officer had stayed behind and he knew they were with us. I didn't want them in the house because of what it would mean later. I didn't dare say the wrong thing and give Dad any chance to take revenge on Mum, the kids or me.

Mum had been crying and didn't ask questions as the male officer looked at us.

'We need to talk to you,' he said.

He was tall and skinny with dirty, fair hair. I led him

and the woman into the living room, knowing they'd see the filth, smell the stench, and wonder how we could live like this.

'As you know, your son Simon has made some very serious allegations,' the officer said. 'We need to talk to you about them.'

Still Mum didn't speak. It was as if she'd lost her tongue and I knew she was so silent because she was scared – scared of saying too much and giving Dad a reason to hurt us when he got home; scared of saying too little and losing her children.

'What's Simon said?' I asked.

'He's alleged that your father threatened to kill him,' the man said. 'He's too afraid to come home.'

I didn't speak as the officer shifted forward in his seat.

'He says he and your siblings have been abused by your father for years and that he has beaten and neglected you all. Simon claims your father watches pornography on the TV, keeps weapons that he threatens you all with.'

Mum sat still. To a stranger, her look might be one of disbelief but I knew different – it was fear.

'He also says that the baby you are carrying is your father's,' the officer added.

My heart pumped as I heard those words. There was a roar of noise, screeching and insistent in my head. Simon knew about Dad and me? About the baby? My stomach swooped as panic filled me. I didn't want Mum to hear this.

'It's not true,' I cried. 'The baby's dad is an old friend of my brother's.'

The officer sat forward as I shrank back in my chair.

'I know this is difficult, Alice, but we're here to help you,' he said. 'There are things we can do to protect you, measures we can put in place if you decide to talk to us.'

I couldn't speak as Mum lifted her head.

'There's nothing to protect us from,' she said angrily.

'Your son seems to think there is.'

'Look, officer, I don't know why he started this but I'm telling you: there's no problem here. I want to see my children and I want them home. You can't take them from me like this.'

'We can, because these are very serious accusations and we need to investigate them. But I want to reassure you that if you talk to us, we can keep you safe.'

I caught just a glimpse of Mum's gaze as my eyes shifted to her face but it was enough. I looked at the police officers as they sat in front of us.

'No, you can't,' I said.

The house was so still that night when the police had finally left. Later, they'd search for incriminating evidence but find nothing other than a video of *The Blue Lagoon*, because The Idiot had securely hidden anything likely to cause him trouble. For now, it was just Mum and I in the the house, and apart from those long hours when I'd been locked in with Dad, I'd never known it so silent. I longed to see the kids, to know how they were and where they were. Would Charlie go to sleep for strangers or Laura be good for them? I knew they'd be crying for us, missing home because it was all they knew. I wanted them back with us, cuddled up to me in bed and away from these strangers circling like wolves. I had to do just as Dad had told me, say what he wanted, and then they'd leave us alone and the kids could come home.

'Is it true?' Mum said as she broke the silence hanging heavy between us.

'What?' I whispered.

I did not want to talk about it. I knew Mum couldn't bear it if she knew the truth.

'Has he touched you?'

'No,' I cried. 'No.'

'Are you sure, Alice?'

'I've told you. It was Michael's friend.'

'So where does he live?'

'Near the shops.'

'Well, you need to tell the police so that everything can be sorted out.'

'I have. You heard me today. And I'll tell them again. I won't give them a reason to keep the little ones from us.'

Mum didn't say any more and I was glad. I didn't want to unlock the secrets we'd held between us for so long. She had enough to deal with now the kids had been taken because she knew what social services could do if they wanted to. I told myself Simon couldn't know anything for sure. I just had to keep quiet otherwise the police would take me, punish me and lock me up.

The following day, the male police officer came to speak to us again and once more we insisted everything was all right – Simon was just making all this up to spite Dad. Later that afternoon, we were allowed to visit the kids at a social services centre for an hour. I felt sick as I walked into the room wondering what they knew about all this.

Mum burst into tears as Charlie and Kate ran up to us, full of questions and wanting hugs. I looked at Laura stand-ing quietly. The look in her eyes cut through me. She was angry and I was sure she was blaming me for everything.

'Why can't we come home, Mum?' Kate pleaded as the meeting came to an end.

'You will soon enough, love,' she replied. 'Just as soon as this is all cleared up.'

Shame rose in me as I looked at all their faces — so lost and lonely. This was all my fault: if I hadn't gone out with Simon, or got a stitch and let him rub my tummy, then Dad would never have attacked him and we'd still be together at home. The children started crying as we got up to leave and asked when they'd be back home. I knew they felt like I did when I was little — scared of Dad but loving Mum. It's amazing how much children love what they know, however bad it is, and they wanted to come home to Mum and me.

'Why won't they let them come back to me?' she sobbed when we got home. 'Do you think we could convince them to, Alice?'

'I'm not sure,' I said, feeling the guilt scratching at the back of my throat.

'But we've got to!' she cried. 'We have to get them back.'

Mum sat silently for hours staring into space and I didn't disturb her as I wondered what was going to happen to us all. It felt as if the world was crowding in on us and, after all the years apart from it, I wanted to be shut away again. I felt so afraid now someone was trying to get into my prison because getting a glimpse of freedom after so long in a cage was scarier than I'd ever imagined. I'd always thought that if someone from outside realised what was happening it would mean freedom and happiness, not this — the kids locked up in social services and Mum at home breaking her heart. I wanted to shut the box back up again and go back to how things had been. At least then I'd understood my world and strangers hadn't been trying to tear it apart. Surely this would all be cleared up soon if we did as Dad told us.

As I sat thinking, I felt the baby move inside me. No one must ever know about it. I must keep silent and then every-thing would be all right.

'They're not going to give them back, you know,' Mum said eventually as we sat in the dark while the TV burbled softly in the corner.

'What do you mean?'

'The kids. They won't let them come home now all this has been stirred up.'

Mum started to cry as I took her hand.

'Don't say that,' I exclaimed. 'They'll be home with us soon enough.'

She looked at me through her tears.

'Maybe it's for the best,' she said softly. 'At least they won't be hurt any more.'

We looked at each other. It was the first time she'd ever said anything like that and one word from Mum, one gesture to show she wanted to get out of this house, and I'd tell my secrets. I just needed her to show me that she understood and would help me run far away from here if I told my story. Then we could get the kids back and live alone with them. It would be just as I'd dreamed – The Idiot would never find us.

'Why don't we just tell?' I whispered. 'Why don't we just talk to the police?'

Mum stared into the darkness outside the windows.

'You know why, Alice,' she replied. 'Because he'd come after us.'

The police returned the next day to ask if I would go with them to look at photographs of local men. They wanted to see if I could identify the father of the baby and the tall officer was waiting for me when I arrived at the station. I wanted to get home as soon as I could because we'd been told Dad was going to be released that day without charge because the police had finished their questioning so they had to let him go while they carried on investigating. I didn't want Mum to face The Idiot without me – he was sure to be asking questions, ready to fly off into a rage if she said a wrong word.

'How are you feeling, Alice?' the detective asked as I sat down. 'How's the baby?'

I looked away. Now more than ever, I didn't want to talk about what was inside me.

'We've got some news,' he continued. 'We want you to leave home for a little while like your brothers and sisters.'

'What do you mean? I can't leave Mum.'

'A legal order has been issued to make you a ward of court. That means you won't be able to go back to your parents for now and you'll be going into a children's home while we carry on looking at this.'

'You can't arrest me,' I said, feeling panic rising. 'I have to look after Mum. She's not well. She needs me.'

'We want to keep you safe but we also want to know the truth so for now this is best.'

'But I've answered all your questions,' I cried. 'Simon's lying. He's making it up. Dad's never hurt us. The baby isn't his. Just let me go home. Let me get back to Mum. Why won't you listen to me?'

'It's only for a couple of weeks, Alice,' the detective said. 'You're nearly eighteen and when your birthday comes you'll be an adult and able to do whatever you like.'

But that was weeks away and I didn't believe him. The police were going to take me away for ever and lock me up. The man was going to question me until I broke down and told him the truth. Then he'd make sure I was punished.

'We can't keep you after you turn eighteen,' the detective continued. 'You'll be free then to do as you wish and social services won't have any authority to keep you in foster care. But for now we are going to look after you.'

The officer got up and opened the door. They were coming to get me. I started kicking and screaming. I had to get home. I couldn't stay here. I couldn't leave Mum all alone with him.

'You can't do this. Please, please, don't do this. Let me go.'

Dad would think I'd said something and take it out on Mum while I wasn't there. He'd kill her just as he'd promised to. I had to get away from here. I'd seen her cuts and bruises so many times over the years. Now he'd do something so much worse. I must get back to Mum.

But hands held on to me and I lashed out as I was pulled, screaming and crying, out of the station into a police car.

'You're going to hurt yourself,' I heard a voice say. 'You'll see your brothers and sisters soon. Stop struggling. What about the baby? You don't want to get this upset.'

But I didn't want to listen. These people were lying. They weren't going to keep me safe. No one had ever protected me before so why would they start now? I had to get home because without me, Mum would be at Dad's mercy.

CHAPTER ELEVEN

I was taken to the same children's home as Laura, Kate and Charlie but even though I was glad to be with them, I couldn't stop thinking of Mum. I pictured the knives hidden under the bed, the crossbow on the top of the cabinet and the throwing stars. Even though I was away from The Idiot for the first time in my life, his reign of terror was as strong as ever. Being in the outside world terrified me because I hadn't got to know it like other girls of my own age. When they were learning to become independent, I'd been shut up caring for my brothers and sisters; when other girls had started going out alone, I wasn't even allowed to walk to the shops by myself because I was not trusted. I didn't understand the real world and felt so afraid now I'd been pushed into it. At least at home, Dad had kept his eye on me and known I hadn't done anything wrong. Now I wasn't there, I knew his imagination would run wild. Without me to watch over, his mind would be filled with fantasies about all the different ways in which I was betraying him and he would make sure he punished me for them all.

The home was noisy, full of screaming kids and social workers who kept trying to ask questions as they spoke to each of us on our own over the next few days. Again and again, they asked me about our life at home: the porn videos, the weapons, the days without food, the filthy house, the knives and slaps.

'We understand you're often alone in the house with your father.'

'Is there anything you want to tell us about your baby, Alice?'

'Is it true your father often watches pornography in front of you?'

'Does he use knives to threaten you with?'

Over and over, they asked about my pregnancy until I wanted to scream. I didn't want it mentioned and I would never talk about the thing inside me. That's all it was – not a baby – but they wouldn't see and it made me feel sick when they kept talking about it. The tall detective also came back, each time trying to convince me that he could keep me safe – Dad would be locked up if only I made a statement about what had happened to us. The police needed evidence to charge him and the detective told me he wanted to take some blood from me and Dad. When the baby arrived they'd take blood from it too. But I refused to help him. He didn't know what Dad was like. How could he? How could anyone? Mum was at home alone with him and if I did anything to get The Idiot into trouble then he'd told me what he'd do.

'It was a friend of my brother,' I kept repeating. 'My father has never touched me.'

Most of the time the officer was patient; there was kindness in his eyes as he tried to persuade my secrets out into the open. But sometimes I could see frustration snap into his face when I kept denying what he knew.

'Alice, please,' he'd say with a sigh. 'Just talk to me. We know what's been happening.'

'No, you don't. Simon's just making this up. Please, please let us go home. Our mum needs us. You don't understand.'

How could I even begin to start unravelling all that had happened with people I'd known for just a few days or weeks? I'd been taught to fear anyone and anything so that's how I felt — hardly daring to speak let alone start confiding in anyone. I knew it wouldn't just be Dad who'd get into trouble but me as well. I didn't want to think about what the police would do to me.

The kids seemed confused by what was happening but not too scared. Laura, though, seemed angry from the moment I arrived at the children's home and tried reassuring her that we'd be home soon. She was twelve and understood far more about what was going on than the little ones.

'What do you know?' she screamed as we fought a few days after I arrived at the home. 'They're going to keep us here and I just want to be with Mum.'

'Me too. But they won't keep us for ever.'

'Of course they will. They can do what they like.'

'No they can't. We'll be home soon. We just need to stick together and they'll let us go.'

Laura's eyes burned as I spoke.

'Shut up, you stupid cow,' she screamed. 'What do you know? This is all your fault.'

'What do you mean? How's it my fault? I wasn't the one who ran away and went to the police. It was Simon.'

'I don't mean that, do I?'

'So what are you talking about?'

'It's all your fault for getting pregnant.'

Guilt surged up inside me. What did she mean? Did she know too? Did everyone know my secret?

'Well, it wasn't by choice, was it?' I screamed without thinking.

The words hung in the air between us. They had rushed out of me – the first time I'd even hinted about what had happened. I stared at Laura, feeling sick, trying to push down the voice which wanted to flood out, the scream inside my head. She turned and walked away. I wanted to run after her but couldn't. I knew she was right. It was my fault.

We didn't speak after that and a couple of days later I was moved to a foster carer's home. I was sad to leave the kids behind but relieved as well that I wouldn't have to look at their faces. I wanted my feelings of guilt gone, buried deep – just as I'd learned to do during all the years when Dad had hurt me. I couldn't stop thinking of how Mum was. I just wanted some news but no one would answer my questions. The foster carer was a very kind lady who made me drink a pint of milk a day because I was hardly eating but her kindness did not sink in. I hated it when she talked about the baby. She didn't understand that I couldn't care less what happened to it. I felt disgusted if it moved inside me and looked away when I caught sight of myself in a mirror. If it wasn't for this baby then none of this would be happening. I'd still be at home and Mum would have her kids with her at least. Now she had nothing.

Once again, the tall detective came back to see me and I asked him anxiously how Mum was.

'A bit down,' he replied. 'She's wondering what's happening with you all.'

I almost told him everything that day. I just wanted it all to end, to be free and go home, to believe the people who told me Dad would be locked up if only I spoke out. But I couldn't find the words and so I stayed silent. I knew I had to do something to find out more about Mum so I decided to sneak home. I was terrified because I hadn't seen The Idiot since he was taken away by the police. Would he know that I'd kept my mouth shut or would he be angry with me? But I knew I had to at least try to find out how Mum was. My heart beat as I knocked on the door and waited.

'Alice!' my mum cried as she let me in.

I walked into the living room where Dad was sitting. He looked terrible – unshaved and dirty – but relief flooded over me as I looked at Mum. She was pale and quiet but not bruised and broken.

'So you're back, then?' Dad snarled. 'Where the fuck have you been all this time?'

I told him what he already knew – that I'd been at the foster carer's.

'It's the first time I could get away,' I said.

As Dad started firing questions at me, I turned to look at Mum. Suddenly I saw everything I'd prayed I wouldn't in her eyes. They were flat and lifeless, there was not even a spark of light in them. She'd lost hope, she didn't care any more what he did and she'd let him do whatever it was he wanted because she had given up now the kids had gone. It was all my fault.

'Get over here and tell me what you've been saying,' Dad yelled. 'What have those little shits been telling those do-gooders? What have the police been asking?'

'Nothing,' I said. 'We haven't told them anything. The police asked to take blood from me but I refused.'

'What do you mean?'

'They wanted a sample. They said they'd take one from you, one from me and one from the baby when it comes. I told them they didn't need to because Simon's lying.'

'And what did they say?'

'They weren't happy but I knew you wouldn't want me to do it.'

'And so why the fuck are the little ones still with social services if you're not talking? Why haven't they come home? You must have done something.'

'I haven't, Dad, I promise. I haven't done anything wrong.'

'You'd better not have or you'll be sorry,' he snarled. 'I want those do-gooders off my back and the kids back here.'

The Idiot sat and glowered in the corner for the rest of my visit – staring at me and asking questions about what I'd been doing.

'So you'll be out of foster care in a few weeks, then?' he spat as I got up to leave.

'Yes.'

'Well, keep yourself in line while you're there.'

He glared at me and once again I knew what he was telling me. Mum might be safe now but not for long if I opened my mouth. I turned to hug her goodbye. I didn't want to leave her. Dad's eyes burned into me as I left and his words ran through my head as I walked back to the foster carer's.

In a few weeks I'd turn eighteen and he knew what that meant – I'd be free to run as far from home as I wanted. But how could I? I had a baby growing inside me, Mum was at home, the kids were in care – everything was such a mess. How could I ever leave it all behind? The detective had kept trying to tell me that it could all turn out all right but I knew different. I could never go against Dad. I was on a leash and every time he tugged, it just got tighter. I would never be free until I knew Mum and the kids were safe. I stared down at my swollen belly as I walked along the road and knew just one thing for sure: I had to be there for Mum.

I had to go home when I was released from care. I had to protect Mum because she wasn't going to look after herself. That was all I thought about as I walked along the road but what I didn't realise in that moment was that I was about to give The Idiot his most precious gift yet: the knowledge that I'd chosen to return to my prison. Now he'd know that as long as he had Mum, he had me.

CHAPTER TWELVE

Dad smiled as he felt the baby twitch.

'That's him turning around,' he said as he moved his hands across my stomach.

'How do you know it's a boy?'

'Because of the way you're carrying.'

He stared at my naked chest.

'Your milk will be here soon. It's not long now.'

I pulled away from him. The only time The Idiot's voice softened was when he talked about the baby. He'd hardly said a word when I walked back into the house the day I turned eighteen. Mum had a faint bruise on her face and seemed as lifeless as ever. But just to make sure I didn't get any ideas, The Idiot had ripped up a benefits cheque a social worker had helped me collect. He didn't want anyone else meddling with my money because it belonged to him – even if it meant destroying a cheque.

'How dare you let them interfere?' he yelled. 'Your money is nothing to do with those bastards. Did you think you were going to keep it?'

'Of course not. They just took me to collect it.'

'That money's due to me so don't try any of your tricks. Do you hear?'

'Yes, Dad. I know.'

The abuse had started again now I was home even though my stomach was big. Once again, I closed myself off from it, sensing that Dad was on the edge now and ready to snap. He was constantly alert for any sign of betrayal, suspiciously asking questions as he waited for another knock on the door from the police, and more watchful of me than ever. Paranoid and on edge, he kept the front door locked all the time and only let Mum and me out to go to the shops and back.

A few weeks after I got home, the police had come again to take Dad away for questioning and he'd ranted about one particular policeman when he was released. The Idiot was sure this officer was out to get him and although I didn't know if it was the kind detective who'd spent so long trying to convince me to speak to him, it was obvious that Dad hated this man, which only made him meaner.

I hardly left home now. Dad drove Mum and me to the supermarket once a month and otherwise I was only allowed out to get bits we needed at the shops every now and again. He wanted to know where I was and what I was doing every second of the day and made me move from the bedroom upstairs that I'd shared with the girls to a box room off the lounge so he could keep an even closer eye on me. If I went to the toilet, he'd shout for me after a couple of minutes; if I took too much time making his cup of tea, he'd holler. Day after day we sat together, as naked bodies flickered on the TV screen and Dad barked orders at Mum and me.

I knew he was thinking about Simon – raging that the kids still weren't back and someone was getting one over on him. A few weeks after I got home, I walked into the living room to find out he'd written a statement for me that he wanted me to copy and give to the police. It said Simon had raped me and that he was the father of my child.

'This will set the cat among the pigeons,' he'd sneered. 'It's called a preventative measure. If Simon wants trouble he can fucking have it. That little shit has got this coming to him.'

Mum stared at us and for a moment it looked as if she was going to speak but then she sat down again.

'What are you doing, you stupid bitch?' Dad snapped. 'Get up off your fat arse and get me a cup of tea.'

She walked out the room and he beckoned me forward.

'Just remember: you'll be in just as much trouble as I am if anyone ever finds out about your baby. You know that, don't you? Now copy the words out in your own writing.'

I sat down in a chair and took the pen and piece of paper he handed me. After I'd reproduced his words in my own handwriting, he read it through.

'There are spelling mistakes in it, you stupid cow. Do it again. You can't get a fucking thing right, can you?'

Later I was sent down to the police station to hand in the letter and the tall detective read it before speaking to me.

'Why have you only reported this after Simon made an allegation against your father?' he asked.

I stared down at my huge tummy. I'd be sent to prison if I didn't do as Dad said.

'I was scared,' I whispered.

I didn't like telling the lie and to be honest I don't think the detective believed me. He didn't say it straight out but I was secretly relieved when nothing ever came of the letter and Dad's attempt at revenge failed.

Meanwhile, Mum was like a ghost – so withdrawn it was as if she wasn't there any more. I knew she was thinking of the kids during the long hours when she sat silently staring into space. I missed them too now I was back at home. The house was so quiet and there was nothing to do without them. Picking up after them, sorting out their food and cuddling them in the night had kept me busy but now the days seemed endless as each hour dragged by.

Mum and I pinned our hopes on the kids coming home as we set about painting their bedrooms. We wanted to make things nice for when they came back to us and Dad allowed us to do it because he'd do anything to get the little ones back. It was a question of pride after all – he might not really want them but he didn't want anyone else getting them either – and, of course, money. The precious child benefit he'd collected for each of the kids had gone and money was tight now. As the weeks passed, The Idiot had got angrier as he counted out every penny and examined shop receipts to make sure the change we gave him added up exactly to what we'd spent. If a penny was missing, we knew we'd be for it.

Mum and I painted the walls of the girls' room lilac and put up wallpaper with pictures of pirate ships and castles for Charlie as we talked about the day they'd come home. We both knew Simon wouldn't be allowed back but I knew the hope of getting the little ones returned was what kept Mum going because it was the same for me. I'd look after her until the kids came home again and the house was filled with their life once more. I didn't even question whether they'd be safer away from Dad. I just wanted to be with them more than anything in the world.

Sometimes I caught myself thinking of the baby as we decorated, wondering what it would be like when it arrived. But I stopped myself as soon as the thoughts came into my head. Remembering how it had been brought into the world, I would hate it again and pretend to myself that the day would never come when it would be born. I couldn't think about it or imagine holding my baby in my arms, knowing it was his. I knew now that The Idiot wanted this baby to be the first of many because he'd told me we'd have more kids after it came.

'What?' I gasped.

'Your mum can't have any and I want more so you're going to give them to me.'

I refused to think about what he'd said as the baby grew. I felt like a prisoner inside my body as well as the house now and nothing – not even a visit from my brother Michael – could free me. He'd arrived one day a few weeks after I got home from foster care and I had no idea who was waiting for me when I went to answer a knock at the door. Standing outside was the brother I hadn't seen for six years. He looked so different to the young man I remembered. He was all grown up now with a powerful chest and longer hair, a beard and moustache.

'Michael?' I whispered.

I couldn't believe he was actually here – so close I could touch him after all this time.

'All right, sis?' Michael said as if he'd never been away. 'I've heard about what's happening with the kids and I'm here to see Dad. Where is he?'

'In the lounge.'

Michael walked into the house bold as brass and I turned to follow. Nerves filled me. What was he doing here? What would Dad do? It had been so long but I knew his hatred for Michael was as strong as ever.

'Hello, Dad,' my brother said as he walked into the living room.

The Idiot stared up from where he was lying watching TV.

'What the fuck are you doing here?' he hissed.

Dad shot me a look as I stood in the doorway. His eyes were black and his mouth twisted into a sneer. Mum sat motionless on the sofa as if she could not believe that Michael was actually real. He walked up to kiss her before turning to Dad again.

'I've come to talk about the kids,' my brother said.

'What do you mean?' The Idiot snapped.

'I've heard about what's going on. I know the kids aren't here and I want to have them to stay with me.'

'What the fuck are you talking about?'

'I need your permission if they're to leave the children's home. They shouldn't be there when I could be looking after them. The social workers say the kids can stay with me while this is sorted out.'

'Are you joking?' Dad screeched. 'Do you think I'd let them go with you? You're not having them.'

'Why not? It would be better than a children's home.'

'Never,' Dad screamed. 'Over my dead fucking body. Do you think you can walk back in here and start laying down the law, you little bastard?'

'I just want to help.'

'You? Help? You're nothing but a piece of shit, like a bit of dirt on the floor that needs to be swept up. You're nothing to us.'

I stared at Michael. Anger and sadness jostled on his face as he and The Idiot started screaming. Mum and I kept quiet, knowing we might get a slap if we spoke up, until Michael suddenly turned to look at me.

'Is it true what they've been saying?' he shouted. 'Is it his?'

'Don't be fucking ridiculous,' The Idiot roared. 'How dare you? Get out! Get out now!'

'Not until I've found out the truth.'

'Fuck off, you little bastard,' Dad screamed. 'Do you hear me? Get out!'

But Michael did not move and I stared at him, feeling the words bubbling up inside me but not moving into my mouth. The anger I knew so well as a child was filling the air once again between Dad and Michael. I felt so afraid of what my brother might do if he knew, so ashamed of how disgusted he'd be by me. It had been so long since we were children and he'd promised to protect me.

'Don't worry about this prick, Alice,' my brother said, his voice soft. 'I won't let him touch you. He won't get past me. Whose is it?'

'Pete's,' I replied.

'Pete – as in Pete whose sister I went out with years back?'

'Yes. I met up with him. It was just a couple of weeks.'

'Really?'

Michael did not speak as he looked at me. I could see uncertainty and confusion in his eyes.

'Yes,' I told him as The Idiot started yelling again.

'How dare you!' he roared. 'Get out of my house.'

Michael turned and looked at Dad.

'Let me take the kids and give them a home. I'm twenty now – old enough to look after them. I'll see them right.'

Suddenly a burst of hope flared up inside me. Michael had come home just as he'd always said he would. Surely he'd take me with him too? I'd persuade Mum to come with us and wouldn't we be safe? It would be just as we'd dreamed when we were kids.

Dad sniggered as he looked at Michael.

'Why should you have them?' he sneered. 'They're not even your proper brothers and sisters.'

It was as if a shutter had slammed down in Michael's eyes. I saw the hurt flash in them for a moment before rage poured out of them again.

'I don't give a shit what you say,' Michael yelled. 'I know who my mum is and they're my blood. Just give me the little ones.'

'No fucking chance,' Dad barked.

There was no way The Idiot was going to let Michael get

his hands on any of us. When the shouting finally ended, Mum and I huddled around Michael – desperate for news of how he was now, what he was doing. He stayed long enough to tell us that he had a girlfriend and two young daughters. I felt shy as we spoke to him – seeing in Michael the boy I'd loved so much but not really knowing the man.

'Let me know if you need anything, Mum,' he said as he left. 'You only need ring and I'll do it.'

He turned to me.

'Look after yourself, sis,' he said.

Nothing more was said about what Simon had told the police and I'm sure Michael didn't ever really think it might be true because some secrets are too terrible to even consider. He promised to phone more often now and I hoped he would because part of me still dreamed that somehow my big brother would come back to rescue Mum and me. Only then would I think about telling him my secret – when we were far away from here and safe. Until then I'd wait. I couldn't leave without Mum.

I was over eight months pregnant when I realised I hadn't felt the baby move for a few days. Everything had been fine when I'd had a scan a few months before but I'd recently missed one because Dad wouldn't take me and now I wondered if something was wrong. I tried to remember when I'd last felt the baby move but couldn't – it must have been at least a day ago but I didn't want to think about it too much. For the next couple of days, though, I was alert, trying to feel the baby inside me – any kind of sign that I wasn't imagining its stillness. I'd got used to it wriggling around and the baby was so big now that sometimes I could see a lump in my tummy where an elbow or foot was resting; it scared me because even though my due date was just a couple of weeks away, I still could not think about what was going to happen. Sometimes I'd remember the kids as babies and the feelings I'd had for them – even when I was tired and they woke me in the night or cried for hour after hour, I had still loved them. But I was sure I could never feel anything like that for this baby. I could not imagine how I would look Mum in the eye every day carrying it in my arms, feeding it and washing it as she helped me.

'I need to go and see the doctor,' I told The Idiot when I first realised how still the baby was.

'And run into the welcoming committee?' he snapped. 'The police will be there and I don't want any more questions. You're fine and that's the end of it.'

It went on like that for three days as I asked Dad repeatedly to take me up to the hospital because I was sure something was wrong. But it wasn't until the fourth morning that he finally took me and I was shown into a room where a doctor started examining me. After a couple of minutes, he turned to look at me with a serious expression on his face.

'I cannot detect a heartbeat. I think your baby has died in the womb.'

'What?' I said, my voice thick and my head rushing.

'I said I think your baby has died in the womb.'

Anger was the first thing I felt – anger that this doctor was so blunt and cold, as if what was happening to me was nothing. But then I remembered: wasn't this what I'd wanted all along? Relief flooded into me as I realised I wasn't going to have this baby after all. I didn't want to think about what The Idiot would do to me. The baby had gone now and that was all I'd asked for. I felt nothing inside, just numb.

I was told I would be given an injection to start my labour because the baby was so big it had to be delivered naturally.

Pain filled me as the contractions started and Mum held my hand as agony ripped into me. I tried to switch myself off from what was happening. I just wanted it over. But then the pain would come again and I'd have to remember what I was doing: expelling the baby he had put inside me.

'Try to breathe, love,' Mum kept whispering.

I knew The Idiot was waiting outside. My teeth sunk into Mum's hand as another contraction started.

'Keep pushing,' the doctor told me.

It seemed to last for ever. I kept pushing and pushing, trying to make the pain stop but it wouldn't. Over and over the contractions ripped through me as I heard the doctor telling me to keep going until the pain burst one final time and there was silence.

'It's a boy,' a voice said.

I turned my head away. I didn't want to see him for a second.

That night the doctors gave me something to help me sleep but my head was filled with cries as soon as I closed my eyes. I saw children in my dreams – Charlie and Kate as babies, faces looking up out of cots and wanting me to comfort them. I felt numb as I lay in the grey morning light and knew that I was empty inside now. I'd got what I'd wished for. The baby had gone. Now maybe all the trouble it had caused would be over and the children could come home.

When the police came to request blood samples once again, I refused them, and also told the doctors I didn't want a post-mortem done on the baby, just as Dad had told me. I wanted to forget all about this baby that had nearly been. But as the days passed, the world felt thicker around me, as if every breath and movement I made was through concrete. It was as if there was an invisible screen separating me from Mum when she came to see me and I could see the tears in her eyes. What had been inside me was real to her, she thought I'd lost something, and while I kept telling myself I hadn't, I couldn't stop thinking of the baby. I had named him Jonathan and wanted to scream when I thought of him. Why did I feel so sad? I'd wanted this, wished desperately for the baby to disappear and now it had. Jonathan had died because of me. I'd killed him just as I'd wanted to all the time he was growing inside me.

Mum took me home when I was released from hospital but The Idiot had decided he didn't want to be around too much while the police were asking questions so he spent a lot of time out in his van. I tried to avoid him, unsure of what he'd do to me now I was home, but I couldn't keep away for ever and Mum told me to take him some food a couple of days after I got out of hospital. He was hiding in his van parked down the road as I knocked on the door.

'Get in,' he hissed as he climbed back into the shadows.

Fear filled me as I saw him. What was he going to do? Would he be angry that the baby had gone? Did he know Jonathan had died because of me? I'd wished for it again and again and someone had listened.

'Where's your mother?' The Idiot barked.

'Inside,' I told him. 'I've brought you some food.'

'I'll have it later,' he said as he pulled the tray out of my hands and flung it down on the floor of the van.

Without a word, he climbed into the front and started the engine. As we started moving, I knew what he wanted from me. Crouched in the back of the van, the minutes passed until I felt it shudder over rough ground and come to a stop. We were parked in a lane somewhere.

The Idiot turned around to face me before climbing back over the seat.

'Please, Dad, no,' I said softly as he came towards me.

I could not bear this now. I could not let him hurt me again. It had only been days since I'd lost Jonathan. I didn't want him near me. I was sore and weak, filled with pain as I thought of my baby.

'Shut up,' Dad growled. 'Get your skirt off.'

As I felt his hands pull at me, I tried to turn my mind off just like I had before. But all I could think of was the baby, my baby, the little boy I'd named Jonathan. Instead of falling into nothing as Dad started touching me, I couldn't get Jonathan out of my head. I hadn't seen or held him. I wished I had. Maybe then I'd have been able to say sorry – for hating him, for wanting him dead.

'Has your milk come through yet?' The Idiot asked as he crouched in front of me.

'No,' I whispered.

He leaned towards me and the smell of sour sweat rushed over me. I stared down at his dirty fingernails, his hair hanging in strands around his face.

'Lying bitch,' he hissed. 'Look at your top.'

I lowered my eyes and saw a wet patch on my chest: milk for the baby I had lost.

'Take off your top,' Dad hissed.

I stared up at him. Surely he couldn't want it? He wouldn't do this to me?

'What do you mean?' I whispered.

'I said take your top off, or do you want a fucking smack?'

His eyes bored into me as I slowly lifted up my top and took off my bra. As he lowered his head to my chest, my mind at last went blank. I knew just one thing now: I'd killed my own baby and Mum had lost the kids because of me. I was rotten inside. This was my punishment. My father was my punishment and he would be for ever. It was all I deserved.

CHAPTER THIRTEEN

We got to see the little ones just once a fortnight at the children's home and each time we left they clung on to us as they asked when they could come home. We could never tell them because we still didn't know. The children were subject to a care order and there was no sign of them being returned to us even though the police hadn't pressed charges. I didn't know if they would do so in future but for now Dad was safe. Even so, he was determined to make things as difficult as possible for the social workers because while he might have been scared of the police, he was more than happy to get the kids doing his dirty work for him.

'Don't listen to a word those fuckers say,' he'd tell them. 'And don't do anything they ask of you: if they want you to go to bed then tell them to fuck off, if they want you to eat their food then throw it at them. You've got to make their lives difficult so they see they can't mess with us. We're not going to listen to a fucking word they say.'

The kids, of course, did as The Idiot instructed them: they were violent, disruptive and caused mayhem in the children's home. Dad even encouraged them to run away and a few times there was a knock on the door and I opened it to find Laura standing on the doorstep.

'That's right,' Dad would laugh as she walked in. 'Let's see if those bastards can find you now.'

Eventually either the police or a social worker would come out to take Laura back but each time she ran away felt like a victory to The Idiot because he'd got one over on the people he hated so much. Within months, he was banned from attending access meetings and the social workers told Mum that she was only allowed to see the kids without him. Dad was furious. Spitting hatred, he kept requesting to see the little ones – as much to waste the social workers' time as anything else I think. But they saw through his pleas, knew he'd never do anything for the children except use them as puppets for his own hatred and didn't give in to him. So Dad refused to drive Mum to the access meetings because if he couldn't see the kids then neither could she and it was more than she dared to try to see them alone.

Now it was just the three of us – Dad, Mum and me – locked into the house and Mum turned in even more on herself when she stopped seeing the kids. I knew she was upset but I couldn't help her because I was just as lost as she was now. I couldn't stop thinking of Jonathan – aching for him in a way I'd never known before, a deep, searing pain which confused me because how could I feel sad for a baby I had never wanted?

The doctor had put me on even more medication but it didn't stop the shame paralysing me and I didn't care what happened to me because I'd killed my own baby. I'd hurt Jonathan and Mum had lost the kids because of me – I was as bad as Dad had always told me. He never mentioned the baby, though, it was as if Jonathan didn't exist until the day a letter came from the hospital telling me there was going to be a ceremony for him. In the envelope was Jonathan's death certificate and The Idiot started grumbling as soon as he saw it.

'Jonathan Peter? Why didn't you give him my name?' he hissed. 'What's wrong with my fucking name? Change it.'

He held up a pencil which I took before sitting down on a chair beside the bed and carefully writing his name on to the certificate.

'There you are, Dad,' I said as I lifted it up to show him.

'Piss off,' he yelled as he grabbed the paper and threw it at me.

I picked it up off the floor, knowing I'd find a place secret enough to hide it. It was all I had to remind me of my son.

'Can I go to his funeral?' I asked as I looked at Dad.

'Can you fuck?' he sneered. 'The police will be there, won't they? There's no way you're showing your fat, ugly face. Now get the fuck out of here.'

The day came and went when Jonathan was buried and I could only think of him as I sat at home with The Idiot watching me. Weeks turned into months and I felt as if I was going to die – numb and in pain at the same time. From the moment I opened my eyes to when I closed them again at night, I couldn't stop thinking of my baby. How would I ever forgive myself for what I'd done?

I thought over and over about Jonathan and the life I'd taken. The tranquillisers and painkillers I'd been given couldn't crush how I felt and I stole some of The Idiot's pills to take with them. I wanted to kill myself and never wake up again but when The Idiot realised what I'd done, he started keeping all the medication in a carrier bag by his bed so he could keep an eye on it. It didn't stop me from wanting to hurt myself though and I started sticking pins into my legs to cause blisters or cutting myself – once gashing my right arm so badly using a piece of broken glass from a bottle Dad had thrown at me that I had to go to hospital where a nurse packed the wound with gauze. When I looked at the scar I'd made, I knew I'd never forget Jonathan and after that used razors to cut myself on my lower arms or ankles. As I watched the blood run out of me, I knew Dad had been right all along: I was bad through and through and there was just one good thing left that I could do with my life – look after Mum.

But just as something had died in me, she had also lost a part of herself. Without the children, she wasn't the same. There were no smiles or hugs, no laughs or whispered jokes. She just sat on the bed beside The Idiot for hour after hour as he ordered her around. When he slapped her or threw something now, she didn't even flinch – just stared at him with empty eyes.

'What's wrong with you, you daft bitch?' he'd scream, trying to see the fear in her face that he enjoyed so much.

Dad just got lazier as he made us do more for him than ever before. By now he didn't even bother going to the toilet and instead used a commode which had been given to Mum because she found getting around increasingly difficult. But Dad decided it would save him some effort so he'd sit on it as we watched TV before making one of us empty it out when it got too full.

It was as if nothing could touch Mum now that she was losing hope. As the months passed without the children, it became obvious that the social workers would never allow them home, even though the police hadn't charged Dad with anything. Mum longed to have the kids back but towards the end of 1989, more than a year after they were taken from us, we were told they would never come home. By now we knew they wouldn't even be kept together because they'd already been separated: Kate was living with a foster family who wanted to adopt her, which Dad refused to allow; Simon had moved to a home in another city and Laura and Charlie were also still in homes.

Something finally snapped in Mum when she realised her children were scattered and she was losing them for ever. After being so silent and withdrawn since they were taken, she now started talking about them all the time – pleading with Dad to allow her to see them even though it made him angry and earned her more slaps. But Mum didn't stop asking Dad for his help in getting the kids back until one night when he finally snapped.

'Can't we just try to get them home?' Mum asked for the hundredth time. 'Can't I go to them and see what happens?'

'You stupid bitch,' Dad yelled. 'You're never going to get them back, can't you see? And why do you want them anyway? Remember what they've said about me? It's their own fault they're where they are.'

'They didn't say anything, I promise you. They just want to come home.'

'Liar. Who was it that told the social workers about the videos? It was those little brats. I don't want them back here.'

Mum looked at him.

'I do,' she said quietly.

He stared at her.

'I've been thinking about how we could do it,' Mum said in a rush. 'Maybe if you left for a few weeks then I could get the little ones back here.'

'What?' The Idiot hissed.

'It would just be for a while and then you could come home.'

Dad's face darkened as he looked at Mum.

'Don't ever fucking suggest that again,' he yelled. 'How dare you tell me to leave?'

'But I can call the social workers, tell them you've gone, then the little ones can come back.'

I felt so scared for Mum as I listened to her. She mustn't fight him, he wouldn't let her get away with this.

'Shut up,' he screeched. 'Or do you want a smack?'

But still Mum wouldn't stop.

'Listen to me,' she pleaded. 'I can get them back and then you can come home once they're here. It needn't be for long – just until the social workers have left us alone.'

As Mum stood up to plead with him, The Idiot grabbed a hammer and flung it at her. It caught Mum on the leg and she started crying as she fell on to the carpet.

'Please listen to me, we've got to get them back,' she sobbed.

'Get the fuck out of my face, you dirty bitch,' he snarled.

Finally Mum was quiet but I knew The Idiot wouldn't let her get away with answering him back like that in front of me. That night I heard soft moans coming from the living room. It wasn't the shouts or screams I was used to. These noises went on for hours, like the cries of an animal, and I got up the next morning expecting to see Mum with a black eye or split lip. Instead, she was covered all over her skin – up and down her arms, at the side of her neck and down her body – with livid red pinch marks. It was different from anything I'd seen before and, while I didn't know what The Idiot had said to her, I knew it was enough to make sure Mum never mentioned trying to get the children home again.

For years after, I wondered why she'd stayed after finally realising that Dad would cost her her children. There was a time when I thought it was because she loved him but slowly I came to realise I was wrong. Mum might have loved Dad when she was a teenager who didn't know any better, but years on it wasn't love that she felt for him, it was hate. She despised him but was too scared to see a world outside Dad. Fear was what bound Mum to her torturer — just like me.

'Alice,' Dad yelled. 'Get in here now.'

He'd just sent Mum out to the shops and my heart started pounding as I walked into the living room.

'Take off your underwear,' he spat as he saw me.

I looked at him. I couldn't bear him to touch me again. Ever since Jonathan, I'd wanted to scream and scratch at him when he told me to get on to the bed. Why was he doing this? He knew I was his now. Surely he couldn't enjoy me lying dead beneath him?

'What are you doing?' Dad hissed as I stood looking at him, feeling as if my legs were filled with lead because I couldn't move to take a step nearer to him.

'Are you listening?' The Idiot said as he got up off the bed. 'Do you know how many pieces I could chop you into? How your mother would scream? And do you think anyone would hear?'

I held my breath as he walked towards me.

'Because they wouldn't listen even if they did hear, you know,' he hissed. 'Can't you see it? No one wants to help you, no one wants to listen to you or see you. You're worse than useless and if you think you can disobey me then you're wrong.'

I longed to see him dead and later that day stole some of

his sleeping pills to crush into his tea. Sitting quietly, I watched him as he sipped. Would it be enough to finish him off? Would Mum and I be free? But, of course, the pills didn't seem to have any effect. Nothing I could do would ever make a difference.

CHAPTER FOURTEEN

I must have been about sixteen when The Idiot discovered how much he liked karaoke. Most of the electrical gadgets he was obsessed with were thrown in a heap in one of the bedrooms – old video recorders, TVs, stereo systems – along with the thousands of video tapes he bought with the benefit money he raked in thanks to all us kids. He also used it to buy a karaoke machine, which he'd plug in at night and sing along to as we lay in bed listening to his howls. His favourite songs were Jim Reeves' 'Put Your Sweet Lips a Little Closer to the Phone', 'In the Ghetto' by Elvis or anything by Hank Williams. Of course, after the little ones left, he was short of money because all the child benefits had gone. So to try and get more he made me go to the doctor to ask about being registered disabled because then I'd earn him more money. But, I was turned down so he kept every penny of the benefits Mum and I collected to spend on himself and bought a machine he could record his voice on – listening back and smiling as he heard himself.

But in early 1990, Dad discovered something he loved even more than karaoke after deciding he'd had enough of where we were living. We weren't getting the kids back and there was no point staying where we were any longer. I knew Mum felt the same as I did: we didn't want to leave the kids behind. But it had been eighteen months since they were taken into care and The Idiot was decided. He told Mum to phone Michael to ask if we could stay with him for a while. He often did things like that – fell out with people for years then swallowed his pride if there was something in it for him. That's what he did with Michael and I knew my brother would agree to let us stay because of Mum. He couldn't say no when she asked him for help and I think part of him also hoped he'd be able to persuade her to leave Dad.

'I'll get you away,' Michael would sometimes say after we moved back to the city where I'd been born and into the two-bedroom flat he shared with his girlfriend Julie and their two young daughters. 'I'll get you a proper home.'

But I knew Mum would never ask Michael for help. At first, I wondered if it was because she felt as if she deserved to be punished for losing the kids – just like I did about Jonathan. But then I realised that the reason she didn't want to let Michael help her was because she knew what The Idiot might do to him if he did. Mum didn't want to bring that kind of trouble to Michael's door. He'd escaped and had a real family life now. His two little girls were beautiful: two-year-old Paula with her dark hair and eighteen-month-old Jacqueline who was redheaded. They reminded me so much of Laura and Kate that it sometimes hurt to see them. That's why Mum would never ask Michael for his help – she knew he was happy now and wouldn't ruin that for him.

I'm not sure what my brother and Julie made of me when I moved in. I was so withdrawn that I think they, like all the people in the years to come, just presumed I was a bit strange, a bit of a recluse. Overweight and quiet, I blended into the background, always aware that I mustn't provoke The Idiot. While living with Michael, he introduced me to some family, including Mum's nephew Sam. But apart from quick hellos and goodbyes, I didn't get to know these people, stayed hidden with my secrets, and no one looked too closely because they didn't think there was anything to see. I'm sure they all thought I was just a shy young woman and didn't know that I stuck to tea when the others had a Christmas drink because the memory of sneaking some cheap sparkling wine years before had stayed with me – Dad had given me a smack and I'd never dared try alcohol again. It was the same during all the weeks we stayed with Michael: even though we weren't alone in the house, I knew that I couldn't cross Dad.

A couple of months later, we moved into our new council flat and The Idiot was immediately up to his usual tricks. He and Mum slept on a sofa bed in the lounge while I had the bedroom off it – which meant he could keep a constant eye on me – and once again the front door was kept locked. Days blurred one into the other as the world closed down to the four walls we sat within. I worried about Mum more and more because her health was getting worse. She was going to hospital more regularly and a couple of times an ambulance had come out to get her. I did what I could, of course, but knew that however many pills she took, it wouldn't be the angina, thyroid or high blood pressure problems that would overwhelm her but The Idiot.

We didn't mark birthdays or the passing of time as the weeks dragged on. While The Idiot watched porn hour after hour, I sat imagining I was somewhere else so vividly that I could almost see the pictures in front of my eyes instead of the filthy lounge and my stinking father. But it was then that Michael introduced Dad to something he loved even more than karaoke.

My brother liked going to country and western clubs – places where people dressed as cowboys, line danced and did pretend shoot-outs with guns loaded with blank bullets – and that equalled a perfect night out for The Idiot. At the country and western clubs, he could indulge his taste for guns among people who innocently thought he just liked the Wild West. So he and Michael started visiting the clubs about once a week and Mum and I were left in the flat together. It was the first time we'd been on our own and the only happy hours I'd known since the kids were taken.

After Dad had gone out with Michael, Mum and I would make tea and toast before cuddling up together in front of the TV. She could hardly believe it as she lifted up the remote control and got to pick what she wanted to watch. When I was younger, she'd loved a police programme called *Juliet Bravo* so now she switched on *The Bill* and we watched it together. Or sometimes we'd sit and play pontoon or rummy and laugh as I teased Mum that she was cheating. We were almost giddy in those moments, free of him and his shadow in the corner, watching and waiting for us to put a step wrong. Mum's eyes would light up as she laughed when I teased her and I knew then that I'd been right to stay with her – she wasn't quite beaten yet and one day I would finally persuade her to leave with me. We never spoke about Dad during those hours alone or the fact that I'd stayed after the kids left. I didn't want to spoil those precious moments together with talk of him.

The Idiot might have made up with Michael long enough to accept his offer of a place to stay but things between them were as up and down as ever. It was just as it had been when Michael was a boy: one minute there was a truce, the next they'd fall out amid shouts and threats.

'That bastard's not coming back in this house,' Dad would scream if Mum asked after Michael. 'I've had enough of him this time. That's it.'

But we slowly learned it never was because Michael eventually came back after every row they had. They both had their reasons: my brother wanted to keep an eye on Mum while Dad needed someone to go out with. So an uneasy peace would spring up between them and soon they'd be back out at the country and western clubs together. Of course, their next falling out was never too far away and it was during one of those that Dad decided to take Mum with him to the clubs.

She seemed happy to go out when she was well but Dad still made her even if she wasn't and I was locked in the house. When Michael and Dad patched things up again, I was even taken up to my brother's to watch over the girls while the others spent the evening at one of the clubs. I enjoyed those nights as I pretended it was my home with my children sleeping in the next room. I'd never thought like that before but discovering romance books had changed something inside me. I'd started reading them after sending off a magazine coupon for a free offer. I thought the book might be a way to pass some time. I only left the flat now for about fifteen minutes twice a week to pick up my benefits on Wednesday and Dad's money on a Thursday so the days seemed to last for ever. But I was hooked as soon as I got the first book and soon obtained more – everything else melting away as my head was filled with the stories of doctors and nurses, star-crossed lovers and handsome princes.

When The Idiot realised I was escaping him for a few

precious hours as I read, he made it clear he hated me doing it. But I was determined not to give the books up – they were the only thing that was mine – so I started hiding them under a towel in the bathroom and reading a few pages whenever I went in. I couldn't be out of Dad's sight for too long because otherwise he'd start shouting for me, but a few pages were enough to keep me going. It wasn't just the stories themselves I loved, though, but the feelings they inspired in me. At night I found myself having thoughts I'd never had before – wondering if I might fall in love and have my own family one day. In the two years since Jonathan, I'd been surer than ever that I didn't deserve such happiness. But now new feelings stirred inside me as the books opened a window on to a world I hadn't known before – where men and women felt tender love for each other, where families were happy and safe. I didn't breathe a word of my thoughts, of course, and kept quiet around Dad, but it was enough to have them.

He was too busy with the clubs to take much notice anyway – in fact, he loved going so much that he soon bought himself all the gear everyone wore: fringed shirts, a long black jacket, black dress trousers and a black cowboy hat. He even wore a gun belt and would put it all on at home to practise with his weapons – drawing the gun quickly out of the belt and holding it in front of his face as he stared in the mirror or shot at balloons. I shuddered to think how much he must have dreamed of using one of his real guns while the rest of the people at the clubs were happy with replicas. In fact, about a year after he started going, Dad got someone to convert his replica guns to carry live ammunition. No one knew what he'd done, of course, but it only ignited my fear that one day he'd finally use one of those guns to carry out his threats. The thought of them was always in the back of my mind when he forced me to have sex.

It was after Dad got hooked on the clubs that something unexpected happened when he told me I was going to go with him. I don't remember how it started – maybe Michael wasn't around or Mum was too ill to leave the house – but whatever the reason was he started taking me. I couldn't believe it. He was asking me to go out with him like a real father and daughter. I knew it was better for me if Dad was happy – there would be fewer slaps with the walking stick or things thrown in a fit of temper – but I didn't understand what he was up to and felt nervous the first few times we went out. Hanging around in the background, I'd watch as he laughed and drank with his friends. I didn't dare speak to anyone in case it gave him a reason to be angry with me.

But as time passed I gradually started to think that maybe this time Dad didn't have a plan and found myself actually enjoying those trips. At least I was out in the real world with people. Soon I was going a couple of times a week and although it felt strange because I knew I wasn't free like others were to laugh, drink and talk to whomever I wanted, I found myself gradually looking forward to those nights because for a few short hours I could convince myself that I was free. I got to know a few of the women, they taught me a couple of line dances and I even started taking part in the shooting competitions myself – feeling a burst of pride if I managed to hit the balloons used as targets and heard people applauding me. Dad didn't like it if I did too well, of course, so I knew I couldn't get too good, but I began to feel alive.

It was the first time I'd seen a world like this. I'd never been to a nightclub, disco or pub before. The clubs seemed

exciting – loud and full of people, chatter and smoke – and
I longed to be part of it all for real. Seeing ordinary people –
husbands and wives, boyfriends and girlfriends – living
ordinary lives made me think. These were decent people.
These men didn't hold knives to throats as they barked out
commands or force their daughters to give them sex like
slaves. They had no idea about the monster in their midst
who smiled and joked – making people believe he was just
like them.

But even though I sensed the club regulars would have
been horrified to know what was happening to me, it never
crossed my mind to tell anyone. I was sure they would hate
me and I was too ashamed to admit what had been happening for all these years so at the end of each night I'd be
locked back up, not knowing when Dad would take me
out again.

I knew I was his when we went back to the club but even
so I couldn't help watching the couples around me – seeing
how some laughed and joked while others kissed and cuddled.
The dreams started by the romance books got a little brighter
as the months passed. Dad had always told me no one would
want me because I was a dirty good-for-nothing. But now I
felt little shoots of hope starting to grow inside me and
began to think about a life outside home. Even Dad seemed
to hint that one day I might be free.

'When you're married you'll have to make sure you live
close by,' he'd told me one day.

I didn't understand what he was talking about.

'I won't find a husband,' I replied, making sure I didn't let
him catch me out by falling for his trick.

'Sure you might,' he said. 'But if you did we'd have to
make sure our arrangement carried on just as it always has.'

It made me feel sick to think of what he'd do. I knew that

if I fell in love, I wouldn't want to keep his secrets any more. I'd want it to be just like I'd read in the books. But the more Dad said such things, the more it made me think about the future. After the kids were taken, I'd almost lost hope about ever persuading Mum to run away with me. But now I wondered if I might be able to. Did I dare dream that I'd have my own family one day? I didn't know what to think but was careful about who I spoke to at the club just in case it made Dad mad. He might have been setting a trap for me with all his talk of marriage. He might be testing me and I didn't want to give him a clue about what I was thinking.

CHAPTER FIFTEEN

Everything changed the night I met Jimmy Dean. It was about a year after we moved back to my home city and I was at the club with Dad when I noticed a man looking at me. He was tall and skinny with brown hair and I knew his face because he was a friend of Michael's. My eyes slid over him at first as I looked around the club but when I turned back, I could see he was still staring. He was looking at me as I stood beside Dad who was laughing and joking with his friends.

'Has the cat got your tongue?' The Idiot suddenly hissed.

'What?'

'I said I wanted another vodka. Now go and get me one. Are you in a fucking dream again?'

I felt my stomach tighten. Somehow I knew the man was still watching me and I did not want Dad to notice. I sat quietly for the rest of the night not daring to look at him again, but the next time Dad took me to the club, the man was there once more. I felt a flutter of excitement as I saw him and a few minutes later my stomach flipped as he walked up to me.

'How are you doing?' the man asked.

I liked his smile.

'Fine.'

'I've seen you around. You're a good shooter, aren't you? And dancer too. Do you like coming here?'

My eyes slid nervously to the dance floor.

'I'm Jimmy,' he said. 'Jimmy Dean. I know your brother Michael. And you're Alice, aren't you?'

I stared at him.

'Yes,' I said.

'Well, it's good to meet you. Would you like a drink?'

'No. I can't.'

'Sure you can! What can I get you?'

'Nothing. I'm fine.'

'Okay. So would you like to dance?'

'No. I should go.'

I hurried off and left Jimmy staring after me. I don't know what he must have thought – probably that I was rude at best and strange at worst – and I was sure he'd just forget me. But I knew I wouldn't stop thinking of him. Getting into bed later that night, I thought of Jimmy again. He'd told me I had lovely colour eyes and those words had surprised me. I couldn't remember someone ever saying such a kind thing before.

I didn't stop thinking about Jimmy for the next few days and every time my stomach flipped inside me. I knew I had to be careful Dad didn't notice that I was nervous and excited at the same time. It was strange. I wondered when I'd next be taken to the club and if I'd see Jimmy there again.

'He wants to know if you'll go out with him, you know,' Michael said a few days later when he came to see us.

'Who?'

'Jimmy, of course.'

'No!' I exclaimed.

'Why not? He likes you.'

'You know I can't. What would Dad say?'

'Just ignore him, Alice. You're twenty-one. You can do what you want.'

I didn't say any more. Michael didn't realise how impossible it was. I'd be killed if I so much as looked at Jimmy outside the club. I just hoped that I might see him again and talk to him a bit more. Maybe The Idiot hadn't noticed me talking to him or maybe he didn't mind as long as he could keep an eye on me. It had been months now that I'd been going to the clubs with him so perhaps he was going to give me a bit more freedom. Even so, I knew there was no way I could ever go on the date with Jimmy that Michael was suggesting. Dad's knives were always ready.

A few days after Michael's visit, I heard the doorbell go and went to answer it. My brother was standing outside.

'I've brought someone to see you,' he said, his eyes twinkling as he walked in. 'We've come for a cup of tea.'

I couldn't believe it. Jimmy was walking in behind Michael.

'Hi, Alice,' he said.

What was Michael doing? He knew Dad would be mad with him for bringing someone into the flat. But he didn't seem to care as we walked into the lounge where The Idiot and Mum were sitting.

'This is Jimmy,' he said as Dad glared at him. 'We're only stopping for a few minutes. We'll just have a tea and then we'll go.'

Dad said nothing as he stared at the TV screen. I looked at him nervously as Michael and Jimmy started chatting. I could feel how angry The Idiot was. Someone was going to get into trouble for this.

'How are you?' Jimmy said as he turned to me.

'Fine,' I said quietly.

I glanced up as Dad got up off the bed and walked out of the room. I didn't know what to say to Jimmy. Part of me didn't want to speak to him but another did.

'So what films do you like?' he asked as I sipped my tea.

'I don't get out to the cinema,' I said.

'And what music do you enjoy? I know you like it because I've seen you tapping your foot along at the club.'

'I just listen to Dad's music.'

'That's right,' a voice said.

The Idiot stood at the door, staring down at Jimmy and me.

'Alice likes the same as me, don't you?'

'Yes, Dad.'

'So what do you like?' Jimmy asked The Idiot.

'A bit of this, a bit of that. What's it to do with you?'

'Nothing really. I just wondered what kind of thing you enjoy.'

Dad was silent for a moment as if he was trying to work Jimmy out. But in the end the chance to talk about his favourite subject was too much to resist. No one else could get a word in as he started talking about himself.

'I do a bit of Elvis on the karaoke,' he boasted to Jimmy.

My eyes met Jimmy's for a minute before I looked back at Dad.

'And I like Jim Reeves too,' he added.

We all sat silently and listened as Dad rambled on until eventually Michael and Jimmy stood up to leave.

'See you at the club, Alice,' Jimmy said as he stood at the door.

'We'll be there,' Dad grunted, and I looked at the ground.

I sat in my chair until I heard the thump of the front door closing.

'What was he doing here?' Dad spat.

'I don't know. Michael brought him. I didn't ask to see him.'

'Don't lie to me.'

'I'm not. I've hardly spoken to him. I wouldn't invite him here.'

'Well, you'd better not, do you hear? I will not have him back in this flat, understand? Who does he think he is? Coming here and asking questions, trying to speak to you while I'm sitting here like a fucking prick.'

'Of course, Dad. I didn't ask him up. I don't know why he came. I won't let him in again.'

'Just make sure you don't.'

As I got up to leave the room, The Idiot raised his hand and flung his cup at me.

'Are you listening?' he growled. 'Because you know what I'll do if you're not.'

I tried not to think about Jimmy but sometimes a picture of his smiling face would creep into my mind. Part of me was scared that Dad might read these new kinds of thoughts I was having but I couldn't stop them. I wished I'd been able to talk to Jimmy, find out more about him. But for now it was enough to remember sitting with him in the living room. It was the first time anyone I might be able to call a friend had come to visit me.

I was watched closely for the next few days and The Idiot didn't take me back to the club. But later that week there was another knock on the door and my heart turned as I heard it. This time I was alone. The Idiot had gone out to the shops with Mum.

'Hi, Alice,' Jimmy said as I opened the door. 'Can I come in?'

I was silent for a moment as I looked at him.

'Of course,' I said in a rush.

I don't know what made me rebel in that instant but I did. If I didn't let Jimmy stay too long then Dad would never find out he'd been here again. We wouldn't do anything wrong. How could a couple of minutes' chat hurt? I just wanted to be like every other young woman.

'Hello,' Jimmy said as he walked inside and leaned towards me.

I breathed in – unable to move as I felt Jimmy's lips peck mine softly. It was the first kiss that hadn't been stolen from me.

'It's good to see you,' he said.

'You too.'

We started chatting as we stood in the hall and Jimmy asked about what I'd been doing, whether I'd visited the clubs recently. Time stood still as I spoke to him and a voice whispered inside me: Jimmy liked me, he wanted to see me so much that he'd come back. But then I heard a key in the lock and turned to see Dad walking into the flat. He stared at Jimmy and me standing together for just a second before he started screaming.

'What the fuck are you doing here?' he yelled. 'Did you think you'd get away with it, Alice? Did you think you'd get him in here without me knowing?'

'No, Dad,' I whispered.

'We were just talking,' Jimmy tried to insist as Dad rounded on him again.

'Get the fuck out of my flat,' he yelled. 'And if I ever see you here again then I'll call the police, do you hear?'

Jimmy looked uncertainly at me for a moment before

turning towards the door. I didn't dare look at him a last time as The Idiot started yelling even louder. I knew what he'd do to Jimmy if I made him any angrier.

'I said get out,' Dad roared. 'Get out now before I do for you.'

Jimmy moved towards the door and his eyes met mine for a moment but I looked away as he opened it and went down into the street.

'How dare you?' The Idiot screamed as the door closed. 'Did you think you'd get away with it? Did you think I wouldn't know, you little slag?'

'No, Dad, of course not. He'd only been here a couple of minutes. I was trying to make him go.'

Dad rushed towards me and I felt his fingers grab tight around my throat as he pushed me backwards, pinning me to the wall.

'No, Dad,' I gasped.

I could not breathe. My lungs were bursting inside me.

'Don't fucking lie to me, do you hear?' Dad screeched as he punched me in the chest. 'What have you been up to? Did you shag him, you fucking slut? Is that what you were doing?'

'No,' I gasped.

He grunted as his hand gripped tighter around my throat.

'What the fuck were you up to? Do you think I haven't been watching you all these months? He's just one in a long line, isn't he? I've seen you at the clubs. Smiling and whispering to all the men, letting them look at you. You're just like your mother – a dirty whore.'

His hand smashed across my face and my eye stung as he let go of my throat and I gulped for breath.

'Did you think you'd get away with this? Did you think you'd make a fool of me?'

'No. No. Please, Dad. I didn't mean to do anything wrong. I didn't want to.'

The Idiot pushed me away from him and I gulped air into my lungs.

'Well, you won't get the chance again,' he spat, 'because this time you're going to learn your lesson.'

CHAPTER SIXTEEN

My bruises healed but the tiny flame of hope Jimmy had lit in me was gone for ever. From the moment The Idiot realised another man had shown an interest in me, he was like a bulldog protecting its mate. Snarling and yelling, he kept me at home for weeks as he refused to allow me out to the clubs.

'I'm not taking you. I know what you're going to get up to and I won't permit it. Do you hear?'

There was nothing I could do but pray and I was sure not to show even the tiniest reaction when he spat at me or lashed out. He wouldn't even let me out of the flat now to run to the shops and back so Mum had to do the shopping. I hated it when she returned home and couldn't get her breath back. I know she wasn't well enough for the walk but Dad would get angry if I tried to suggest that I went instead.

'Why do you want to do that, then?' The Idiot would say. 'Are you meeting someone?'

'No, Dad. Mum's not too good. She gets so tired.'

'She's making it up. You're staying here.'

'I wouldn't take long. I'd go straight there and back.'

With a grunt, he flung his walking stick at me.

'Do you think I'm going to let you out like a bitch on

heat? Do you think the local boys wouldn't see you coming? Who the fuck would want you? Look at yourself, you fat, lazy slag. You're not going anywhere.'

Once the front door had often been left on the latch but now Dad insisted it was locked all the time and he was given the keys. He didn't want me letting anyone in or me getting out and the only time I was allowed to leave the flat was when The Idiot made me go down to the family planning clinic to get a pregnancy test. But however much I told him there was no way I could be pregnant, he didn't want to listen.

'You were having that Jimmy when my back was turned, weren't you? And now you're pregnant by him, aren't you? You're like a bitch on heat.'

After two tests, Dad was finally convinced no one had touched me and started ordering me back on to his bed again. I was sure I'd never be given even the tiniest moments of freedom again. His anger was blacker than I'd ever seen it.

Eventually, though, he took me back to the clubs because Michael had moved further away from us by now so we only saw him every few months and Mum was often too unwell to go out. Dad wanted someone to fetch and carry for him so he had to take me but Jimmy didn't say hello when I saw him. He must have realised what a bad lot I was with a father like mine and I didn't enjoy going out any more because I felt so scared all the time. The Idiot took me a couple of times a month and I didn't dare look at a man, let alone breathe a word to one. Dad's eyes were on me all the time – when I got up to go to the toilet, if I bumped into someone on the way, he watched my every move.

'Were you chatting him up?' he'd hiss when I got back to my seat.

'No,' I'd insist. 'I was just trying to get past.'

'Don't lie to me, you little bitch.'

The only man I was allowed to have any contact with now was Gavin, who had the mind of a child. He didn't pose any kind of threat as far as Dad was concerned so I was allowed to dance with him for one song. As soon as the music ended, I'd sit down again wishing I could leave. I didn't want to be at the clubs now knowing that I'd never have what I'd dared dream of.

But however quiet and obedient I was, Dad wouldn't forget what had happened with Jimmy. Even the gas man wasn't allowed into the flat to read the meter any more. What did The Idiot think I was going to do? Who did he think would take any notice of me? I wore shapeless clothes and baggy underwear because he picked all my clothes and they never fit. He was the only man who touched me.

I'd gone back on the pill after Jonathan but stopped taking it because of terrible migraines so The Idiot had to use condoms. Sometimes he did, sometimes he didn't and I knew he'd want revenge for Jimmy. Each month I waited anxiously for my period to arrive – counting down the days until I knew it was due and feeling almost weak with relief when it came. But although it took a long time after losing Jonathan, I eventually realised I was pregnant again and was filled with an even stronger horror than when I was a young girl. I knew now what might happen and hated my body for doing this to me again.

Once again, though, I started bleeding a few weeks later and went up to hospital where I was told I'd miscarried. The Idiot made me sign in under a false name just in case anyone was watching us and I knew he was annoyed with me. I had miscarried three babies now and lost Jonathan – I was as useless as he had always told me. It was the simplest thing in the world to carry a child and I couldn't even do that. The Idiot was never going to give up. Why wouldn't my body give him what he wanted and set me free?

I had learned when we were kids that The Idiot would never back down if there was a fight to be had, like the time he got arrested for attacking a neighbour during a row about an ice-cream cone. Dad never let anyone beat him. It was the same now, all those years later, when he picked a new fight with the woman who lived downstairs with her kids. It started because she liked listening to loud music and Dad would spit with rage when the beat thumped up through the floors and into our lounge, disturbing whatever he was watching on TV at the time.

'Shut up,' he'd scream as he started banging on the floor.

But the woman below didn't seem to take any notice because she never turned down the volume and The Idiot got more and more incensed. A couple of times the police were called when the two of them came face to face and started screaming insults at each other. Or Dad would pick up the phone to them when he'd had enough and just wanted to cause trouble.

'That fucking bitch,' he'd spit as he dialled, 'I'm going to teach her a lesson once and for all.'

Most of the time, though, Dad just turned up the volume on our TV and Apache screams would fill the room as he tried to make the sound of the western he was watching drown out the music below. Our neighbour, though, was nothing if not a fighter and nothing my dad said or did could intimidate her. So as soon as he turned up the volume on our TV, she'd do the same to her music and Mum and I would be deafened by its pumping beats as they fought with the roar of a film.

It went on for months. Complaints were investigated and accusations made as each side vowed to win the fight. However, in late 1992 it came to a head when The Idiot decided he was going to shut her up good and proper. Sick and tired of banging on the floor, he realised he needed to do something extra noticeable and rummaged through one of the boxes of junk he kept lying about the place. Soon he found what he was looking for: a huge bar bell that he'd kept from the days when he weight-trained.

His face went red and his breath came in gasps as he lifted the weight above his head and crashed it on to the floor. I heard a crack as he groaned and lifted the bar bell up again. His cheeks were purple by now but he didn't stop. He lifted the weight once more and crashed it down with a scream.

'If you want some fucking noise I'll give it to you,' he roared.

The bar bell ended up smashing through two of our floorboards, caving in part of the woman's ceiling, and finally the battle was over. Not because the woman was frightened into giving in and turning down her music, but because Dad decided it was time to move. He had shown her who was boss and couldn't be bothered to walk down all the stairs any more from our third-floor flat. We moved to a ground-floor place and I was happy because at least no stairs meant Mum could get in and out so much more easily. Her walking was pretty bad now and she got breathless if she tried to move too much. But she didn't complain and whenever I asked how she felt she'd tell me the same thing.

'I'm okay,' she'd say with a smile. 'It's just a bad day but tomorrow will be better.'

But while our new flat gave Mum a little more freedom,

it only made me even more of a prisoner. Being on the ground floor meant Dad could watch me even when I left the flat now and there wasn't a second of the day when he didn't know what I was doing. I got out of bed when he told me to, went to sleep when he decided it was time and couldn't be in the bathroom or kitchen too long before he started shouting.

I think he got braver because he'd started seeing more of his sisters, nephew and nieces who came to visit sometimes. It made The Idiot feel even stronger because he was part of a tribe again and his sisters looked up to him so much that there were no limits now to the extent Dad wanted to be in control. It was more than four years since the kids had left and Mum was still lost without them but her fight had gone. Sometimes I'd find her sitting in a chair looking at their pictures and tracing the outlines of their faces.

'They're not being hurt any more,' she'd say as she looked at them.

Now Mum and I were the only ones left to order around and we weren't even allowed to speak without Dad's say-so and had to sit in silence for hours while he watched TV. We were his prisoners and fear kept us in chains. I left the flat even less now and being sent to the shops almost scared me as much as being at home because I knew Dad was watching me as I crossed the road. Most of the time the living-room curtains in our flat had been closed with just a crack open at the top to let in a sliver of sunshine because The Idiot liked living in the half light. But now when Mum unlocked the door and I was sent to get some food or cigarettes, Dad would pick up his stick from beside his bed and pull back the curtain to see me. I knew he was watching my every move and my heart hammered as I ran across the road. It happened more and more now: I'd feel as if my heart was going to burst as the breath was crushed out of me. Kneading my sweaty palms, I'd try to tell myself everything was okay. But it felt as if I was going to die when the panic flooded over me and I stood in the shop praying that the person in front would hurry up.

'What took you so long?' Dad would snap when I got home.

'There was a queue.'

'Didn't look like one to me. I couldn't see anyone going in or out of that shop. Were you talking to someone?'

'No.'

'Are you sure?'

'Yes, Dad. It was busy, that's all.'

'Well, just remember I've got my eye on you.'

'I know.'

'And if you dare try anything then I'll finish off your mother, do you hear?'

His threats would ring in my ears every time I left the house and if someone who knew Dad or one of his relatives stopped to ask how Mum was, I'd always be too scared to linger. Muttering a few words, I'd hurry on because I knew that he was watching and waiting – staring at the clock to make sure I didn't take a second longer than he'd put up with and give him an excuse to punish me.

CHAPTER SEVENTEEN

It's hard to know why monsters do half the things they do but I think The Idiot stopped performing even the most basic human tasks for himself because it made him feel powerful when we did them for him. No job was too disgusting, no request too repulsive that Mum or I would dare say no.

The black hole we were falling into just got deeper and deeper in those years after we moved to the ground-floor flat and Dad stopped getting out of bed. The only time he moved was to go to the clubs occasionally and soon he had bed sores – red, weeping wounds on his backside – that people in hospital get. But Dad wasn't ill, just lazy and determined to humiliate Mum and me every second of the day. It started with the bed baths he demanded she give him because his skin itched but soon he even stopped using the toilet.

It was less than ten feet from the living-room door to the bathroom but he wouldn't even take those few steps. Instead, he used bottles to pee in or would crouch over a mop bucket he kept by the side of the bed. Sometimes he'd throw the toilet paper on the floor after wiping himself and my stomach would turn as I had to pick it up. He still spat on the floor, of course, when he felt like it but now his mess was littered across the lounge. Of course, he didn't always hit the bucket and I'd have to clean up after him then too. But if I didn't do it right or if I took too long and got in the way, he'd make sure to let me know.

'Hurry up, you silly cow,' he'd say as he picked up a piece of stained toilet paper and threw it at me.

Once when Michael was visiting, he tried to have a word with Dad as he peed into a bottle when he was lying in bed.

'You could ask us to go out when you do that, you know,' he said.

'When you've got to go, you've got to go,' The Idiot replied with the hint of a smile, as if he almost enjoyed people's shock.

The only thing he'd do for himself was shave because I think even he wouldn't risk letting Mum or me anywhere near him with a razor. Just one slip of the knife and it would all be over. He could sense the danger – just like the night I took one of his knives and stood over him while he was sleeping. My hand trembled as I stared at Dad – just one swift move and we would be free. But he stirred in his sleep as if he knew I was near and I crept back to my room with my heart thumping.

He controlled every move we made and Mum did everything from cutting his toenails to combing his greasy hair. Whatever she did, though, he'd usually end up shouting and as time went by the panic I felt when I went outside started to fill me when I heard his screams. The only time he moved was to throw something at us or scream abuse. There was less physical violence now but the moment Dad began to shout, I'd start to shake. I knew what was hidden in the room with us; I could see the pictures of the weapons in my head even if they weren't in front of me.

'Will he kill me this time?' a voice would shout in my head. 'Will he really do it?'

And then another softer voice would whisper: 'I hope so because then you'll be free.'

There was never any logic to The Idiot's moods – he used any tiny thing as a reason to humiliate us. One night, for instance, Mum and I were sent out in the early hours to get him a takeaway. It was a long walk in the cold and we hurried back, both silently hoping that his food was still hot.

'What's this?' he sneered when he tasted it. 'It's a curry from the fucking Chinese, isn't it? Those fucking Chinkies can't cook.'

'But the chip shop was shut,' Mum tried to say as Dad threw the plate of burning food at us.

Bits of hot sauce spattered my bare arms as I tried to get out of the way and the plate hit the floor.

'Just clean it up,' he snapped. 'And get me something else to eat.'

He didn't care now what bruises he gave us because we hardly saw anyone – not even the nurses who needed to come and visit Mum were allowed in. But while there were occasions when he hit Mum or me, most of the violence was psychological now. He'd learned how to control us without using his fists. Once I walked into the lounge when he was practising with his knives and one flew past my face. It felt as if he was giving me a message. Or he'd lie in bed next to Mum and pinch her again and again. Tiny little nips which made him laugh as he saw her flinch in pain.

'Please stop,' she'd tell him. 'I don't like it.'

'I don't care what you want, you fat, lazy bitch,' he'd sneer. 'You can't look after me right so what the fuck use are you? I should get myself another woman.'

'Maybe you should,' Mum would whisper before he back-handed her across the face and she started crying.

He didn't hit me as much but the worse thing was that he didn't care how much he hurt me when we had sex now. For so long, Dad had almost pretended to be gentle – asking me if I liked it just as he had when I was a little girl. But now he didn't seem to care as he forced his way inside and made me do whatever he wanted. Eight months after moving into the new flat, I fell pregnant again. I was just a few weeks along when I found out in the summer of 1993. Once again, I lied about how it had happened but Dad didn't get away with it so easily this time because his relatives asked questions, even if Mum didn't. I knew Dad's sisters and nieces were whispering about this pregnancy. They were the only people allowed in the house so they knew more than most what my life was like.

'How did she do it? She's never out. I haven't seen her with a boyfriend.'

The Idiot silenced them all with a snarl.

'She's the biggest slag around here,' he'd tell them. 'Look at her, the useless lump. She just takes what she can get. She's done it since she was a girl and it's the same this time. Fucking whore.'

Thankfully, it was only a couple of weeks before I started bleeding again and had another operation. I didn't feel anything when I miscarried for a fourth time because how can you feel when you're already dead inside? There were rocks in my heart now and although Dad was more careful for a while because of all the questions, I knew the time would come when he wasn't.

I was his prisoner and The Idiot knew for sure the night he took me to a Christmas party at one of the clubs. Looking at the families sitting together, I thought of my brothers and sisters and wondered where they were and what they were doing as I remembered the times we'd been together and the fun we'd had. They'd always got so excited about Christmas, desperate for me to tell them about Santa Claus and his reindeer. Did they remember me now? It had been so many years since I'd seen them and yet suddenly it felt like yester-day as I looked around at the families drinking, singing, dancing and celebrating together. Mum and I weren't even allowed to talk about the kids now. We'd received a couple of letters from the social workers after they'd gone but soon it was as if they'd never existed and I felt so sad as I looked at all the people around me and remembered. I knew I had to stay strong for Mum because she was getting weaker and weaker, but it was so hard.

'How about a dance?' a voice said, and I looked up.

The man was tall and handsome with brown eyes. He reminded me of Jimmy.

I didn't think about Dad when I agreed to dance with him or let myself feel afraid about the punishment I knew would come, the beating I'd get. I wanted to feel alive like I had when the kids were still with us – as if there was someone in the world who wanted me – and holding on to this man I could believe it for the few short minutes the song lasted. At the end, he leaned forwards to kiss me and I let him: my first proper kiss. Not the peck Jimmy had given me or what Dad had taken. For a moment I felt life flicker inside me. I knew The Idiot's eyes were on me every second and when I sat down at the table, I felt his fingers dig into my arm.

'What the fuck are you playing at, you stupid slag?' he shouted. 'Do you think anyone would want you or do you think he knows you're the biggest whore in here?'

A man sitting near us looked around as The Idiot threw a string of insults at me. He was a friend of Dad's but now stared at him as if he didn't know him at all before quietly moving away. Dad was usually careful to hide what he was really like from outsiders but he was too angry for that now.

'Will you never learn?' he yelled. 'No one else is going to want you, do you hear? He just knew you were fucking desperate, that's all. All he wanted was a quick poke, do you hear? Now move it.'

He didn't stop screaming for the next hour. In the car and back in the flat, he told me I was a prick tease, a joke and I'd been egging the guy on – desperate to fuck him. Everyone knew what I was like. There wasn't a person in the club who didn't know what a slut I was.

'She didn't mean it,' Mum kept trying to reassure him.

'Don't give me that shit!' The Idiot screamed as he walked up to me holding a knife in his hand. 'She wants to humiliate me in front of all my friends.'

He pushed the blade towards me and grabbed hold of my arm.

'I will fucking kill you if you ever embarrass me like that again,' he screamed. 'I'm not taking you there to get your hole filled, do you hear?'

I stared at the knife in terror as he looked me up and down. I was wearing a new T-shirt he'd bought me, an old skirt and trainers.

'Give me that top now,' he yelled. 'I buy you something nice and then you're all over him.'

I took off the top and handed it to Dad. With a snarl, he started ripping it until it lay in pieces at his feet. Standing in my skirt and bra, I turned towards my bedroom door so that I could get another T-shirt.

'What are you doing?' The Idiot roared. 'Get out of my flat. I don't want you anywhere near me, do you hear? I don't want a little slag like you in here.'

Grabbing at a T-shirt lying on the floor by my bedroom door, I turned towards the hallway.

'No,' pleaded Mum. 'It's freezing out there. She'll catch her death.'

'Good,' The Idiot snorted. 'It might teach her a lesson.'

He pushed me towards the door and I dug my feet into the carpet.

'Please don't,' I shrieked. 'Don't make me go outside. Let me stay here. I won't do it again. I'm sorry, Dad.'

But he didn't listen as he pushed me out into the cold and I heard the key turn in the lock. I didn't want to be out here alone. I knew what was waiting for me. I'd been told by Dad for long enough that the world was a dangerous place.

Sitting down on the step to wait, I could hear The Idiot shouting at Mum as she asked him to let me back in. I shivered as fear filled me. What was he going to do to her? How could I have been so stupid? I should never have done it. Now Mum would get hurt again because of me.

Sometime during the night I heard the footsteps of neighbours coming home from a night out and ran behind the rubbish bins to hide. My heart beat in my ears as I waited for the people to go into their flat. I'd never been outside alone like this before. All I'd done were trips out in the day but hadn't gone out at night by myself. There were dark shadows, I could hear shouts and see the flash of car lights. I felt so afraid. The world seemed so huge now I was in it all by myself.

'Let me in,' I whispered through the letter box. 'Please let me back in.'

The hours slid by and my pleas got slowly louder as I begged Dad to let me inside. I wanted to be with Mum and make sure she was safe. I wanted to be back in my prison.

'I won't do it again,' I called. 'I'll be a good girl.'

It was getting light by the time Mum finally opened the door. She looked as if she'd been crying.

'You're to come in now,' she said quietly. 'Just go to your room.'

That was the moment I knew for sure I was dead inside. As I walked back inside, I heard the door lock behind me and knew I'd never escape.

Dad didn't hit me too often now but, just like when I was a child, it was the fear which was the worst thing. My breath would come in ragged gasps if he moved towards me and, knowing the noise would make him even angrier, I would try to breathe silently. Be as quiet as a mouse. The migraines I'd had since I was a teenager also became worse and I took more painkillers to try to stop them but nothing worked. Sometimes it was up to fifteen paracetamols a day – far too many and a dose which could have really hurt me – but they didn't dull the pain. It felt as if my head would split in two but I wasn't allowed to go to bed until Dad told me I could. Sometimes it was three or four in the morning before he finally switched off his porn films and so I just had to sit there, waiting and wondering when he'd come for me next or let me finally go to bed.

It was always Mum who got it worst. It must have been a couple of years after we moved into the ground-floor flat that he punched her so badly in the jaw that she couldn't speak properly for days. She tried to tell me that it wasn't too bad but I could see the bruises and a bulge on her jaw line. I was sure it was broken.

'You've got to go to hospital and get it seen to,' I said one day when we were in the kitchen.

'It's fine, Alice. It will settle down soon.'

'Please, Mum,' I begged. 'You've got to tell him how bad it is and make him take you to the hospital.'

'Honestly, love, it's fine. It feels better already.'

Mum wouldn't listen to me however much I pleaded and so in the end I stopped. But it scared me as I wondered how far Dad would go. He didn't seem to care any more, it was as if he wanted to push and push us to the final moment when he finally made good his threats. I watched and waited for trouble to flare again and it did a couple of weeks later when Mum brought his tea and The Idiot flew off the handle the moment he saw the poached eggs on toast she'd made for him.

'What's this? I hate eggs. Why did you give me this?'

Mum was standing by the bed as he tossed the plate at her and it smashed on the carpet. She looked down at the broken egg yolks and china at her feet.

'Those were the last two eggs,' she snapped. 'It was all we had.'

'What did you say?'

There was a moment of silence as Mum looked at him.

'I said those were our last two eggs,' she replied slowly.

'Well, I didn't want them, you dirty cow.'

I tensed as Dad threw back the covers and got out of bed. Wearing an old nightshirt, he lumbered towards a piece of wood leaning against the radiator.

'How fucking dare you?' he yelled. 'Do you think you can answer me back?'

Mum didn't move as I started screaming.

'No, Dad! She didn't mean it. I'll get you something else to eat.'

'Get the fuck out of the way,' he roared. 'Otherwise you'll get it too.'

Raising the wood in the air, he smashed it across the top

of Mum's head. She staggered as she was hit before falling on to the carpet. She looked stunned, as if she couldn't believe what he'd done to her, and Dad clenched his hand into a fist as he stood over her, daring her to try to get up. Mum lifted her palm to the top of her head. It was covered in blood as she pulled it away.

'What have you done?' I cried.

Crouching down beside Mum, I saw blood pouring out of a two-inch gash on her crown.

'We've got to call an ambulance,' I pleaded. 'She's got to get this seen to. Look at her. It's bleeding so much.'

'What are you fucking talking about? It's nothing.'

'Please, Dad. She needs a doctor.'

'No, she doesn't. Now get that snivelling bitch out of my sight or you're next.'

Mum was gasping for breath as I got her to her feet and led her out of the room.

'It's okay,' I kept whispering. 'I'll look after you.'

Mum didn't say anything as we went into the hallway.

'Sit down,' I told her before running to the kitchen and wetting a dishcloth under the tap.

I ran back and started dabbing at the cut. I didn't want to hurt Mum but I had to stop the bleeding. The gash looked so deep and blood was pouring from it. I didn't think I'd ever stop it.

'You'll be all right,' I said as Mum flinched a little. 'I'll sort this out for you.'

It seemed to take for ever until the blood finally stopped running. The cloth was covered in it and I felt light-headed by the time I was finished. Any harder and Dad would have killed her.

'Are you all right now?' I asked as I hugged Mum. 'You're okay now, aren't you? I'm here. I'll look after you.'

She didn't speak as I held on to her. I wondered if she was thinking the same as me. Was he finally going to kill us soon? When would this ever stop?

'Get back in here,' Dad eventually shouted from the living room.

He was back in bed and a horror film was on the TV.

'Sit down both of you and shut up. It's just a fucking scratch. It'll teach you both to cook a proper meal for me, won't it?'

Mum stared at the TV as I looked at her. Turning my head towards the screen, I pushed down the tears which were stinging in my eyes. Weeks later, I woke up to find that I couldn't see properly. There were only shadows and outlines in front of me now when I opened my eyes. I went to see the doctors and they ran all sorts of tests but nothing was found. Eventually I was told there was no physical reason why I'd lost my sight and it was down to stress. After a few weeks my vision started to return but months later it happened for a second time. Once again my sight came back but it was as if my body was trying to blind me to the horrors I saw each day.

CHAPTER EIGHTEEN

In late 1995 I fell pregnant for the sixth time and The Idiot told me to make sure nothing went wrong this time. Mum didn't even ask me how I'd got pregnant and I was almost angry until I told myself that someday soon she'd find the courage to fight. Until then, I'd keep quiet and look after her just as I always had.

As weeks turned into months and my stomach grew, The Idiot told me that this baby would be the first of many.

'Surely you know that by now?' he said with a smile. 'Your mother can't have any more and so it's your job now.'

I wondered if he'd finally leave me alone and the violence would stop if he got what he wanted. By now I knew I'd give almost anything for that and felt disgusted with myself that I almost wanted this baby just to escape. Maybe it was the only way that Dad would leave Mum and me alone. I worried about her all the time. I wasn't sure how much longer she could cope. I had to find a way to help her.

I was sure that I'd lose this baby like all the others but as the weeks turned into months, The Idiot became convinced that all his wishes were finally coming true. He watched me day after day like a cat making sure a tasty mouse doesn't run for cover: ordering me not to lift anything heavy, reading a book about the different stages of pregnancy from cover to cover and making me stand in front of him naked when Mum went out so he could stare at my stomach. Sometimes he'd put his hands on me as he tried to feel the baby move and told me once again that I was going to have a boy. He also said that no one in the family should know about my pregnancy and so if anyone visited, I had to sit in a chair. I was quite overweight by now and, with my baggy clothes, it was easy to hide what was happening. We didn't see many people, of course, and Dad's relatives didn't take much notice of me even if they did come.

As the months went by, I started to feel the baby move and remembered the feelings I'd had when I was pregnant with Jonathan. Back then I'd crushed them down but this time it was harder as thoughts slipped into my mind about what the baby would look like or how it would smile. The pain of losing Jonathan had never left me and now I felt so confused: half of me hating the baby because of how it had come into the world, the other half wanting it because I longed for something of my own to love – just like all the women I'd seen at the country and western clubs.

Mostly, though, I didn't let myself think about the day I might become a mother. I couldn't imagine it ever happening because then my nightmare would finally come true. It had been ten years since I first fell pregnant and time had proved to me that nothing would stop The Idiot except my own body which refused to allow a baby to be born. When I went for a scan at twenty-eight weeks and was told the baby wasn't developing properly, I was sure I was going to lose it. Relief wrestled with shock as the doctors reassured me that they just needed to keep an eye on things more closely.

I told myself they were just hiding the truth as I went home to break the news to Dad.

'What do you mean, it's not growing?' he exclaimed. 'You look fine. You're big and round.'

'The doctors said the baby was too small so I'm going to have to get checked more regularly from now.'

'Well, do whatever they say, do you hear?'

But even though I was sure that history was going to repeat itself, I was wrong. The doctors monitored me, gave me steroids and booked me in for a caesarean at thirty-seven weeks in July 1996. The child inside me was small but alive.

I pushed down a scream as I was wheeled into the operating theatre. This couldn't be happening. It could not be real. I wanted to run and hide, go to sleep and wake up and realise I was in another place. I could not bear to give him what he had forced inside me. I wanted to close my eyes and die. I was in a bright white room, filled with eyes looking down from behind masks, faces I was sure could see my secrets.

'We won't be a minute, Miss Lawrence, and all you'll feel is a few tugs before your baby is born,' a woman's voice said.

I didn't know who was speaking and didn't dare reply to the eyes looking at me. They seemed so cold, as if they knew the truth. I knew what they were telling me. A head leaned close to my ear and I heard another voice.

'You'll be right, Alice. It'll only take a jiffy.'

Dad was standing beside me and I turned my head away as he spoke. I didn't want him here but he'd insisted on attending the birth. He had to see his precious baby born. I felt sick as I thought about how much he was going to enjoy seeing the doctors cut into me. I'd told them the baby's father was a landscape gardener who was working away. They'd never suspect in a million years that he was standing in the room with them: my father, my baby's father; my sibling, my child. But I knew what they'd say if they did know.

'How could she let it happen?'

'Dirty slut.'

'Sick bitch.'

The Idiot leaned forward and I looked at his hand resting on the white sheet beside me. I pushed it away as the doctors started the caesarean but he didn't notice as he stared over the screen hiding my stomach. Revulsion filled me as he watched, excited as a schoolboy in a sweet shop. I hated him and I hated his baby which was coming into the world. I knew that now. There was no love inside me. All the years of my pain would be bleached into its bones, every slap and punch would mark it out; this baby would be cursed for ever just like me. I felt tugging and pulling on my stomach. I wished I could close my eyes and it would all disappear.

'It's a girl,' I heard a voice say.

I held my breath waiting for a cry, the sound which would prove to me she was real. I was a mother. I remembered the silent seconds after Jonathan was born as a nurse gathered up the bloody bundle and carried it into an adjoining room.

'What's happening?' I cried. 'Where are you taking her?'

'Not to worry, Miss Lawrence. She's a little bit drowsy. We're just warming her up.'

A son and now a daughter. They were both so silent. She was just like him. My two lost children.

And then I heard it.

A cry.

A wail.

A scream which filled me.

And in that instant I knew my baby could never be my curse. She had not asked to be conceived. She was my daughter, a tiny, innocent child whom I must protect for the rest of her life.

'Well done,' I heard Dad say and a feeling I'd never had before rushed into my veins. I would never allow my daughter's father to hurt her as he'd hurt me.

I called the baby Caitlin and it was three days before I could finally hold her because she was so small and weak. She hadn't been breathing properly when she was born and had to have a blood transfusion. When she was transferred to intensive care, she lay in an incubator covered in wires and I said silent thanks that she had survived.

'She's beautiful,' Mum said, and I looked away as The Idiot smiled.

He had what he wanted now. After all these years, he'd finally got it – another baby. I wanted to fly at him and scratch out his eyes as he leaned towards the incubator where Caitlin was lying and told me how gorgeous she was. He sounded like any other proud grandfather. But he wasn't and we both knew it. I just wanted him to go, to leave me alone to stare at Caitlin lying so tiny in her cot. A rush of love flooded into me as she moved a little and her fingers flexed.

The doctors still didn't know what was wrong with her. All they knew for sure was that Caitlin was weak and couldn't feed properly so a tiny tube had been put into her nose as she lay in the incubator. I knew that she'd get stronger, though – she'd survived for a reason – and I promised to stay with her day and night. She was so tiny that she almost scared me. It had been so long since I'd looked after Charlie and Kate and now I was too scared to even touch Caitlin.

She was so fragile. What if I hurt her? The nurses, though, showed me what to do and I was allowed to dress and cuddle her as I learned how to care for a baby once more.

A few days later the doctors told me I was well enough to go home but Caitlin was going to have to stay longer at the hospital because she was still being fed by a tube. I didn't want to leave but had no choice and felt empty when I walked back into the flat. I was back in my prison while my daughter was lying in a hospital cot so far away. I could not stop thinking of Caitlin all alone. I just wanted to be with her. For a moment after the front door was locked behind me, I felt afraid as I wondered if The Idiot might not let me go back to her now I was home again. But I'd kept telling myself while I was in hospital that he couldn't stop me and knew I had to remember that now. Caitlin needed my milk which I was going to express every few hours before taking it up to her in bottles each day.

'You'll be able to apply for child benefit now,' The Idiot said on the first morning after I got home.

'What?' I asked.

It was the last thing on my mind. I hadn't stopped thinking of Caitlin for a second and wanted to leave for the hospital as soon as possible.

'You'll be able to get a payment for her now as well as your own benefits.'

'But I've got to go and see Caitlin. I haven't got time to go down to social services.'

'You have and I'm taking you,' Dad snapped. 'We've got to get the baby's money sorted out.'

I knew it would be easier if I did as I was told so I sat quietly as The Idiot drove me down to the benefits office where I filled out the forms without thinking.

'Is there anything you can give me while we wait for the

money?' I asked as I got back into the car. 'I haven't got anything for Caitlin. I need clothes and a pram for when she comes home.'

'So you're going to cost me even more now, are you?' he snapped. 'I'll see if I've got any spare cash but it won't be much. A baby's not supposed to cost, you know.'

I didn't know what he meant and didn't care because soon my days fell into a rhythm of visiting Caitlin and willing her to grow strong. Sometimes I even spent the night with her and although The Idiot got angry, he knew there was nothing he could do to stop me. Caitlin needed me and he wanted her home as soon as possible so whenever he grumbled, I had the perfect excuse to leave the house. It was as if having her had switched a light on inside me: everything had changed because I had a job now that even The Idiot couldn't stop me from doing. Instead of being locked in the house all day every day, I had to go out to do things.

'Where are you off to now?' he'd snap as I put on my coat.

'To the shops to get Caitlin some nappies.'

'What the fuck do you need to go out for again?'

'Because I have to get things for the baby.'

He couldn't stop me and I'd feel a surge of excitement as I slammed the door and stepped outside. I'd been so afraid for so long but the love I felt for Caitlin was making me stronger. Day by day, week by week, I felt a little braver. Of course, I was still scared but, as long as Caitlin was in hospital, Dad had to let me leave the house. She was my reason now to get up in the morning and live. The days which had been so grey suddenly had colour as I left the house and walked to the bus stop before the twenty-minute ride to the hospital. After getting off, I'd walk up the steep hill and feel fresh air blowing on my face. Some days it was cold, on others it was pouring with rain, but I didn't care because I had a place to go now.

I was out in the world for the first time in years and couldn't believe how many types of people there were. I'd never been into the city before and tried not to stare as I saw people with multicoloured tights and hair, women with pierced noses and eyebrows. The other thing I couldn't get over was that quite a few people had mobile phones. I'd seen them on TV but knew they were very expensive. Looking around me, I'd walk up to the hospital and feel excited that soon I'd be with Caitlin in the baby unit. I felt like I had a place there – nurses knew me, other mums chatted to me, I was 'Caitlin's mum'. I was someone now and there was nothing The Idiot could do to stop me from being the best mother in the world.

CHAPTER NINETEEN

I was standing outside the hospital having a cigarette when a woman I knew called Lisa walked up to me. Caitlin had been in hospital for a few weeks now and Lisa was one of the mums I'd got to know because her son Josh had been born with a cleft lip and palate so he needed special care too. I liked chatting to Lisa and the other mums – they almost felt like friends as we talked about our babies and how they were doing.

'How's Caitlin?' Lisa asked as we stood side by side.

'Okay,' I replied. 'She's put on some weight and they're pleased with her. How about Josh?'

'Fine, so they say. But he just looks too tiny for them to be talking about all these operations.'

'I know. I was scared to death when they took Caitlin out of her incubator for the first time so I could hold her. I was so sure I'd drop her.'

Lisa smiled at me before her face turned serious again.

'I just can't stop thinking,' she said quietly. 'Sometimes I look at him and wonder if it's my fault. Was there anything I did wrong? Do you know what I mean?'

'Yes.'

'I just keep thinking about it, running through everything

in my head but I can't find a reason. I don't think I did anything but I must have.'

'I'm sure you didn't,' I said softly.

Lisa stubbed out her cigarette.

'Well, I'd better get back,' she said. 'My daughters will be
home from school at three so I haven't got long. See you up
there.'

I bowed my head as Lisa left. I knew how she felt but
while I was sure there was nothing she could have done to
stop Josh's problems, I knew Caitlin was different. I'd been
thinking about it more and more lately and it was the only
time that my new courage failed me as I stared at her and
the thoughts crowded into my head. Was it my fault she
was sick? Was it because I'd let him bring her into the
world that she was being punished just as Jonathan had
been? I tried not to think about it as I sat beside her each
day and didn't ask the doctors too many questions because
I was so scared of what the answers might be. Lately
they'd started talking to me more about what was wrong
with Caitlin and told me they thought it was a genetic
problem.

'We need to run some tests so we'd like some blood from
you and Caitlin's father,' they said. 'Do you know how to
contact him?'

'No. He's disappeared and I can't get in touch.'

'So you don't have a phone number or an address?'

'No, nothing like that. Nothing at all.'

I gave them my blood, of course, and even asked Dad if
he'd do the same but he refused.

'Couldn't we buy a needle and I'll take the blood up to the
hospital?' I said desperately.

It was a stupid idea, of course, but I wanted to do anything possible to help Caitlin. Wouldn't he do the same? I

knew he couldn't love her, he'd never loved any of us, but maybe he'd help because Caitlin was sick.

'Don't be so fucking stupid,' he snarled. 'That's the end of it, do you hear?'

I gave up trying to persuade him and just kept telling the doctors that I had no idea where Caitlin's father was. The guilt lay heavy as a rock in my stomach, though, just as it had all those years ago when the kids had been taken into care because of me. So many people had been hurt because of what I'd let Dad do and now I was scared my baby was also paying the price.

I told myself Caitlin would get well if I just gave her enough love. She was already getting stronger and slept in a normal cot instead of the incubator. I'd even been allowed to dress her and take her down to the hospital café in a pram a couple of times. But although I felt proud as I wheeled her in front of me, the doctors told me it would still be a while before I could take her home.

The main reason for keeping her in hospital was because of her feeding problems and I had to learn how to tube-feed Caitlin because she couldn't suck a bottle. The nurses had been teaching me how to feed her by threading down her nose a tiny tube which ran into her stomach. It was hard because Caitlin had such a tiny nose and the tube seemed so big as I gently inserted it. When it was done, I had to make sure there was no air in the tube and do a special test to check it had gone into her stomach. Then I'd slowly pour milk from a bottle into the syringe attached to the tube and feed her until she'd had enough.

I wondered if I'd ever be able to do it right and worried Caitlin would never be well enough to come home. I just wanted her with me and Mum felt the same as I did. She came to visit Caitlin whenever Dad would drive her up to the hospital and on the days when she couldn't, she'd ask me questions about what had happened when I got home.

'How was she? Did she have colour in her cheeks?' she'd ask as I sat down.

The Idiot got annoyed as we talked but I wondered if a little of my courage had rubbed off on Mum because she'd chat until he gave her one dirty look too many and she went quiet again. I enjoyed it, though, when we talked about what Caitlin was doing, how pale her skin was, how tiny her feet were. That was what we were doing one day as we sat alone together by Caitlin's cot, when the doctors arrived to ask about the baby's father again.

'I haven't got any news,' I said. 'I just can't get hold of him. He's disappeared.'

'But are you sure, Miss Lawrence? It's very important. It will be very hard for us to diagnose Caitlin properly if we don't have her father's co-operation.'

'There's nothing I can do,' I insisted, feeling the old fear turning in my stomach. 'I've told you again and again that I don't know where he is.'

Mum looked at me questioningly when the doctors left.

'Do you really not know, Alice? Is there nothing you can tell them?'

'No,' I said crossly. 'Stop asking me questions. I've had enough from the doctors.'

Mum didn't say any more until we were sitting on the bus home and she turned to me.

'Caitlin looked well today, didn't she?' she said. 'I'm sure she's growing.'

'Yes. I just wish they'd let her come home. It shouldn't be too long now.'

'It will be good to have a baby in the house again.'

'I know. I hate leaving her. I can't wait for her to be with us all the time.'

My heart ached as I thought of Caitlin back at the hospital. Every time I left her was painful because it didn't feel right leaving her there with strangers when she had a home to go to with me. Mum and I fell silent for a moment before she spoke again.

'There's something I want to ask you,' I heard her say.

I knew what she was going to say without hearing the words. My body tensed as she spoke.

'Is he the father?'

I took a deep breath. It seemed like for ever before I could answer.

'No,' I said. 'No, he isn't.'

Mum didn't say another word and I was glad. I didn't know if I'd have been strong enough to tell her the lie again. I turned to look at her. She was staring blankly ahead, her eyes almost empty as she looked at the road. I knew I'd done the right thing. She didn't want to hear those words. I put my hand over hers and we sat quietly together.

A few days later the doctor came to see me once more and told me they had some news.

'We have done a scan,' he said. 'You must prepare yourself, Alice.'

'What do you mean? What's wrong?'

'I'm sorry, but there's no easy way to say this: we have discovered that Caitlin is brain-damaged.'

I stared at the doctor. What did he mean? Caitlin was perfect.

'We're not sure why it happened,' he continued. 'But it seems her entire brain activity is affected, which means the damage isn't limited to one area. It will affect every aspect of her life.'

'I don't understand. She looks so well, she's growing like she should be.'

'I know,' the doctor replied. 'But although we can't identify the exact cause of Caitlin's condition, we believe it is a genetic problem. It's very serious, Alice, and I have to tell you that the extent of Caitlin's brain damage means she is unlikely to reach puberty.'

I wanted to scream as the doctor spoke. How could he say this to me? How could he know what Caitlin was capable of when he didn't even know what was wrong with her?

'Caitlin is severely brain-damaged and has a limited life expectancy,' I heard a voice say.

My hands started to shake as I bent my head. It was just as I'd feared. The doctor was telling me Caitlin was going to pay the price for my sins.

'But she's perfect,' I whispered.

When the doctor had gone, I bent down to Caitlin's cot. She was sleeping. She looked so peaceful. I reached out to touch her soft cheek. I wouldn't listen to what the doctor had told me. He didn't know anything for sure and I wasn't going to give up on my baby even if he was. What did he know? I'd make sure my daughter survived. She had to live. She was my life now.

CHAPTER TWENTY

I smiled as I wrapped Caitlin in a towel. I'd just given her a bath and was going to put her down to sleep for the night soon.

'Baa baa black sheep, have you any wool?' I sang softly. 'Yes sir, yes sir, three bags full.'

Caitlin made a soft gurgling noise as I patted her dry and bent my head to kiss her. I could never get enough of her smell, so clean and new, and I knew it was true what they said – babies really were a miracle.

I wiped gently around the feeding tube running into Caitlin's nose. I'd been coping well with it since coming home; in fact, the only problems I had were when she was a little rascal and pulled it out. The health visitor, though, told me I was doing a good job because Caitlin was putting on weight just as she was supposed to. But I worried that the health visitor would complain about the pigsty we lived in – row upon row of units filled with Dad's video tapes and covered in cobwebs, the stink of his mess in the living room. I'd been keeping my room as clean and tidy as possible but The Idiot wouldn't let me do anything to the rest of the flat.

'This is where we spend our time,' I told the health visitor. 'We don't go into the lounge too much.'

She looked around and smiled at Caitlin lying in my arms.

'Just try to keep the dust down as best you can,' she said kindly, and I felt as if she knew that I was doing my best.

But I still didn't want her coming to the house too much so if the weather was good enough, I'd take Caitlin down to the clinic to be seen. Other than that, Dad didn't let me out and the front door was locked as always. So I'd stay in the house with Caitlin, cuddling and feeding her, changing her nappy and giving her baths. I didn't mind being locked in the house again – I just loved looking after Caitlin and so did Mum.

'Let me take her,' she'd say if the baby vomited up her milk, which she did a lot because she had stomach problems.

'But she'll make you dirty, Mum. You don't have to do it.'

'Well, it won't be the first time and it won't be the last,' Mum would say with a smile. 'Give her to me for a cuddle.'

Whispering to Caitlin, Mum would gently undress her but a couple of times her hands started shaking when she lifted the baby up and I knew she was almost scared about hurting something so precious. The Idiot, though, screamed if Caitlin cried too much and ranted when his TV was interrupted by the noise, which happened quite often because Caitlin sometimes cried for hour upon hour and it wasn't easy to settle her. It made Dad wild but for some reason he didn't fly at me so much now. In fact, it was Mum who got more of the beatings and insults and I bit my lip as I watched him kicking out her arms from underneath her as she tried to crawl out of the bed beside him or laughing if she had an accident. I knew I couldn't get involved in their fights as much any more because I had Caitlin to look after and I didn't want to give him any reason to get in a rage with me and take it out on her. But I worried for Mum because The Idiot just got meaner all the time.

Having Caitlin home was as wonderful as I'd dreamed it would be during all those long weeks when she was in hospital. I seemed to spend hours just looking at her, staring at my baby's face as I imagined the future she was going to have. I knew I'd make sure she had all that I never did: proper schooling, pretty clothes, the chance to go out with friends her own age. I knew what the doctors had said but tried to forget it, even if they thought I was kidding myself. When I took Caitlin back to hospital for regular check-ups, I was sure she was doing better than they'd predicted. For instance, the doctors had said she wouldn't recognise me but I was certain she did. When I talked to her and tickled her, I knew she gave me little smiles and I was the only one who could soothe her when she cried.

Being a mum made me more tired than I'd ever been in my life before because I had to tube-feed Caitlin every couple of hours whether it was day or night. But I didn't care because it was exciting – the feeling had never left me since the moment she was born. I wasn't just The Idiot's plaything any more and felt as if I'd accomplished something at the end of each day. Before Caitlin, the weeks had slipped one into another as months and then years had passed while we sat silently in front of the TV screen. I was twenty-six years old now and it had been eight long years of darkness and terror since the kids had left.

But now each day seemed different and I knew Mum loved having Caitlin with us almost as much as I did. I could see it in her face as she held her and rocked her. We were always talking about the baby and I was glad Caitlin made Mum smile because it meant that at last I'd given her some happiness instead of all the pain. Even after all this time, the guilt I felt about what happened between Dad and me was as strong as ever. I had betrayed Mum for so long by letting her husband do what he did. I also felt filled with shame as I remembered all my other pregnancies. Now I had a baby, I realised even more how wicked my feelings had been and felt full of guilt at the thought that I had killed my unborn children. But now at least I hoped I might have done something good: I would love Caitlin enough for all my other babies and one day she might be the reason to finally give Mum and me the courage to run.

It was almost impossible to get any money out of Dad to buy the baby what she needed and I had to beg him for nappy money. But in the end I persuaded him to give me a few pounds to buy a cheap cot and pram and Mum and I kept back enough from it to get a couple of teddy bears. At Christmas, I was even given a few pounds to buy Caitlin a colourful plastic half-moon which I hung at the end of her cot. The day was the same as any other – no decorations, no turkey – but she made it special.

Michael was pleased as punch when he came to see her.

'She's beautiful, sis,' he told me and I felt so proud.

It was moments like those when I could almost forget who Caitlin's father was and smile like any other mum. But then I'd remember when I woke up in the middle of the night and the flat was dark and silent. I told myself that Caitlin would never be his, she was mine and I'd look after her properly, make her safe from him. Sometimes Dad would hold her if I was busy cooking or folding the washing but I hated having her near him and would take her back as soon as I'd finished what he'd told me to do.

The doctor's questions about Caitlin's health problems

had rattled The Idiot, though, and he'd started using con-traception again. He must have remembered all the questions from the police when the kids were taken and known that if he wasn't careful someone else would start asking more. So while the sex still happened from time to time when Mum went out, it wasn't as often as before. I didn't complain, though, because I was too scared of what he'd do to Caitlin if I gave him even the slightest reason to get angry. The one thing guaranteed to send him into a rage, though, was money and he'd started pestering me about it almost as soon as Caitlin came home.

'You can apply for disability allowance now, you know,' he kept telling me. 'You can get extra for her because she's sick.'

At first I didn't take any notice. I wasn't thinking about anything like that, just trying to get used to having a baby at home and looking after all her needs. Caitlin had to have regular medication and a monitor was fixed to her chest all the time, which sounded a bleep if her heartbeat slowed down. When it went off, I would rush to her and usually find she'd pulled the monitor off. But once I had to gently massage her heart as I'd been taught to and it scared me so much – as did the seizures Caitlin had started having after she came home. Sometimes I was sure she wouldn't survive because she was so tiny and weak. But Caitlin proved to everyone how strong she was in January 1997 when she was seven months old and devel-oped pneumonia.

The doctors had told me to prepare for the worst when I took her into hospital and I'd spent the night sitting by Caitlin's cot and praying she'd be well again. The next morning I was told she still wasn't over the worst and I asked for a vicar to come and see us. Tears ran down my cheeks as he made the sign of the cross to baptise Caitlin. I couldn't lose her. She mustn't be made to pay for all I'd done wrong.

As I watched and waited for a sign that she was going to pull through, I pleaded with anyone who'd listen to save Caitlin. I knew she was sick and had problems but I'd give her a good life, a happy one, the best I could. It was two awful days before the doctors finally told me she was out of danger and I sobbed when I heard the news. I'd always known that despite all her problems Caitlin was stronger than anyone believed and now she'd shown them.

The Idiot, though, didn't care about any of it: how sick Caitlin was, how much attention she needed. All he was interested in was getting me to apply for disability benefit and he badgered me about it day after day.

'You could get more for her, you know,' he'd say. 'She's ill. She needs care. There are allowances for kids like her.'

Once again, I went down to the benefits office and filled out the forms before posting them and forgetting all about it. But when a letter came through the front door a few weeks later, The Idiot flew into a rage.

'How the fuck can they refuse you?' he screamed. 'Why won't they give her disability benefits? Look at her. Did you fill out the forms right? Did you tell them everything they needed to know?'

Suddenly an anger so powerful filled me that I forgot myself as I listened to him screech.

'Is that all you care about?' I shouted. 'What does it matter? She's a baby. I give you everything I get. What more do you want?'

Dad's eyes bored into me as I sat with Caitlin.

'As much as I can get,' he hissed. 'Now give me the copy of the form you filled out and I'll check what you wrote.

There must be a way we can get those tight bastards to give us more.'

My stomach twisted inside me as I handed him the form. Everything – his kids, his wife, our sicknesses and births – came down to money. For so long, I'd tried to understand why he'd behaved as he had: had I made him, was I to blame, had any other girl made her father do as mine had done? But now I finally realised that as well as the power, terror and control, it was down to money. That was why Dad got so angry when Mum couldn't have more children and why he'd forced himself on to me year after year. We'd been earning him a packet when we were kids and he wanted Mum to keep having his children to get even more. Then as soon as I was old enough, he'd put me to 'work' – raping me to get another child and another benefit cheque. My head swooped as I stared at him. I'd been too stupid to see it. He didn't care what he had to do to get more cash in his pocket.

Dad went through the application form I'd filled out with a fine toothcomb before ringing up the benefits people to rage at them for refusing me more money. But he was told Caitlin was still a baby and therefore didn't qualify. I was happy that he'd been turned down. It would teach him a lesson.

Two months after she recovered from pneumonia, the doctors told me Caitlin needed to have an operation. She was still being tube-fed via her nose and they said it would be better for her to have one inserted into her stomach because it would be less uncomfortable. I listened as they told me and wondered if she really needed to go through something like that. Caitlin weighed fifteen pounds now, which showed that the way I was feeding her was working. In fact, she was so much stronger that I was sure the doctors would soon tell me they'd been wrong to diagnose her as they had. I knew she wasn't like other babies – she didn't lift her head or wriggle around, she didn't coo at me or giggle – but she was my world and, as her mother, I could see the changes in her. The doctors, though, said the operation would make her stronger and I knew I must listen to them. I agreed to have it done and took Caitlin into hospital in late March 1997.

She was going into surgery the next day and I watched as the doctors did all the tests they needed to make sure she was well enough before settling her down for the night. I hardly slept as I worried about the next day and felt so afraid as I dressed Caitlin when she woke up. I didn't want her to leave me as she was taken away by a nurse. My arms felt empty without her, the world was so quiet now she was gone. The doctors had told me the operation would last four hours and they seemed like the longest of my life as I waited for her to come back. Relief washed over me when she was brought back to the ward.

'It went really well,' a nurse told me, and I spent the rest of the afternoon sitting by her cot.

Caitlin slept fitfully for the rest of the day and each time she woke up I'd stroke her hand to let her know I was there. Eventually, about 11 p.m. I gave her a last kiss goodnight.

'Sleep tight, baby,' I said before sitting down in the chair beside her cot.

I couldn't wait to pick her up again and take her home. Caitlin would get even stronger now. We would prove the doctors wrong, I thought as I fell asleep wondering how long she'd be in hospital. But a few hours later I was shaken awake to see faces in front of me, people standing by Caitlin's cot.

'Your daughter is in distress,' a voice said.

'What do you mean?' I cried as I stood up.

'We need you to leave us for a minute, Alice. We have to look after Caitlin now.'

I was in a daze, didn't understand what was happening as hands guided me out of the room.

'But I want to be with her,' I cried. 'Let me stay here.'

'You can't, Alice,' a nurse said. 'The doctors need to look at Caitlin. They'll come and get us when they're ready. We've just got to leave them to do their work now.'

The nurse took me to the smoking room where I lit a cigarette. The smoke tasted bitter as I inhaled it. I didn't want a cigarette. I wanted to go back upstairs. Why wouldn't they let me?

'Please,' I sobbed. 'Let me go back. I'm her mum. She needs me.'

'It won't be a minute now,' the nurse told me.

Tears ran down my face as I waited until the door opened and another nurse asked me to follow her.

'Where's Caitlin?' I cried. 'How is she? Is she okay? What's happened?'

'The doctor wants to see you, Alice,' the woman said as we got into a lift. 'He won't be a minute.'

Panic forced the breath out of me as the lift door opened and the nurse walked me towards another room.

'But I want to see Caitlin,' I pleaded. 'What's happening? Please tell me.'

The door to the room opened and I saw a nurse and a doctor waiting for me.

'Where's my daughter? What's wrong? Why won't you tell me where she is?' I sobbed. 'I just want to see her.'

By now I was crying and shaking. I could hardly stand up straight as the doctor walked towards me.

'I'm sorry, Alice, but there was nothing we could do,' he said.

'What do you mean?' I screamed.

'She was a very sick little girl. We did all we could.'

'I don't understand. Where's Caitlin? I have to see her.'

'I'm afraid we couldn't save her, Alice.'

'Where is she? You said she'd be well.'

'I'm sorry but Caitlin did not survive.'

'What?' I screamed. 'I want to see her. She needs me.'

'Alice, listen to me.'

I felt hands holding on to me as I started to fall.

'Caitlin is dead.'

Everything went black.

CHAPTER TWENTY-ONE

I can't remember anything but glimpses about those days after Caitlin left me: desperate to get back to the hospital because I was sure someone had stolen her, they were hiding her from me, I just had to find my baby and we'd be together again; Michael coming to see me and stopping me from leaving the house.

'Let me go,' I screamed at him as I tried to get to the front door. 'I've got to find her. They've got her.'

'But where are you going, Alice?'

'To see Caitlin. She's at the hospital.'

'She's not there any more.'

'She is. I left her there.'

'Come with me. You can't go out now, Alice.'

'Let me go. Please let me go.'

Eventually Michael took me to see the doctors at the hospital where Caitlin had been treated because I wouldn't stop asking for her.

'Where is she?' I cried. 'Who's got her?'

'She's not here,' a man told me.

'She is! She's having an operation. She'll get better. They told me she'd get better.'

'I'm sorry but Caitlin has died, Alice. She's not here any more.'

'I don't understand.'

'She's gone.'

'Where is she? Where's my baby?'

In the moments when I wasn't sedated, I pleaded with people to help me before everything went black again. Even Caitlin's funeral was a blur. Later I was told that when I dressed her for burial in a white smock with pink bows and a white cardigan, I lifted her up, held on to her tightly and didn't want to let her go. Apparently my parents, Michael and some of the doctors and nurses who'd looked after Caitlin were at the ceremony but I can't remember them watching me as I ran forward to try to grab the casket when the hearse doors opened or later when I screamed as the coffin disappeared behind the crematorium curtains.

The first clear memory I have is of waking up in my room alone and wondering where Caitlin was. I couldn't hear her breathing and everything felt so silent. Then Michael walked in.

'You're awake, sis?'

'Yes,' I said as I sat up and looked around me.

Caitlin's cot was empty.

'I've come to get the child benefit book,' Michael said gently. 'It has to be returned.'

I looked at him and remembered. Caitlin had gone. She wasn't with me any more.

'I haven't got it. Ask Dad.'

Michael closed the door and I lay back down again. That's all I can really remember of that time – the feeling I had then: emptiness and a slicing pain in my broken heart. I couldn't believe I was alone again. I just wanted her back. I wanted Caitlin with me.

Life was meaningless now. Without my baby there was no reason to carry on, no point to anything, and I sat for hours staring into space. My life with The Idiot and Mum went back to how it always had been: I was locked in the flat and allowed out to go food shopping or twice a week to collect the benefits. The only change was that Dad paid for driving lessons for me. He didn't even want to get out of bed now to drive Mum to her hospital appointments.

'I'm sick of being a fucking chauffeur,' he told me. 'You can run her around. You've got nothing else to do.'

It was as if Caitlin had never even existed: I was given an hour to leave the flat, queue at the post office for our money, pick up doctor's prescriptions and get them filled out at the chemist. One minute over and The Idiot would start asking questions and each time I got home he'd check the mileage on the car because it was a two-mile round trip. But I didn't care because I didn't even think about trying to get away any more. Without Caitlin, there was no point to anything; without her, I did not want to carry on. For so long, I'd thought about escaping and hoped that some day Mum and I would finally do it. But now I knew I'd never have a normal life because I'd destroyed my own daughter's. I was a monster.

The doctors said Caitlin had died of cot death but I knew it was because of me. She had paid with her life for my mistakes. I'd given birth to her and consented to the operation. I was supposed to protect her and instead I'd let the doctors do what they wanted and now she'd gone. I'd allowed The Idiot to get me pregnant and Caitlin had been punished for it. I couldn't stop the thoughts whirring away in my mind as I sat for hours each day holding a picture of her. Sometimes her face would blur in front of my eyes but I didn't look away for a moment. I felt dead inside. Each moment of each day hurt me because I knew Caitlin was not with me.

The only person who understood was Mum. She'd lost children too and knew how it felt. Mum missed Caitlin almost as much as I did and sometimes we'd sit crying together as we looked at photos until The Idiot told us to shut up. At night, I'd lie down holding a picture of Caitlin and one of her cuddly teddy bears. It was white with a pink hat and I'd laced Caitlin's hospital tag around the ankle. Lying in the dark, I'd turn it around and around as I tried to sleep. But I couldn't stop thinking. Caitlin had paid with her life for all that I'd done and I knew my sentence was to be a prisoner for ever.

The months passed and I became like a shadow – not moving or flinching when Dad slapped me, which made him even more vicious. I didn't care what he did any more and that meant he didn't have the pleasure of sniffing my terror in the air or seeing it on my face. If he threw something at me, I didn't move; if he hit me, I stared at my feet and if he screamed abuse, I turned my head to the wall.

By the time 1997 drew to a close, Caitlin had been gone for nine months and I was as withdrawn as ever. The Idiot still took what he wanted, of course, but I was like a dead thing and he didn't come back too often for sex. I didn't care though. He could do what he liked with me now just as he'd always done.

Michael started visiting more after Caitlin's death and sometimes brought the girls with him. They were so grown-up now – Paula was ten, Jacqueline was nine and they were like a streak of lightning in the darkness. I knew Mum loved them visiting because we hadn't really seen the girls since those few months seven years before when we'd lived with Michael. Now Mum lit up whenever she saw the girls but I didn't. Nothing could get through the grief which had buried me alive.

'I'm worried about you, Alice,' Michael told me when he came to visit at Christmas. 'Why don't you come and stay with Julie and me for a while? It might do you some good.'

'You know I can't,' I replied.

'Why not? Mum will be fine.'

He just didn't understand.

'Come on, Alice. There are too many memories here. You can stay as long as you like.'

I looked at him. Was he remembering the promise he'd made all those years before when we were children sitting on a bed and he'd magicked bread into biscuits and water into lemonade? Surely he knew it was too late now? Jealousy stabbed into me as I watched Michael leave with his daughters. They were a family, just as I had been with Caitlin. I knew I'd never stop wanting to be a mother for as long as I lived. Caitlin had changed me for ever. She'd shown me life beyond my prison.

'You stink,' The Idiot snapped as Mum handed him a cup of tea. 'Have a fucking bath, won't you?'

I stared at the TV as I heard Mum leave the room and the taps being turned on in the bathroom.

'What's up with you?' Dad said. 'Sitting there like a fucking moron, not speaking or moving.'

I could feel his eyes on me.

'Get over here. Your mum will be a while yet.'

I didn't move.

'I said get over here now.'

I knew what he wanted. I wouldn't give it to him.

'Are you fucking deaf or something?'

Still I didn't move.

'Do as I tell you or your mum will feel the back of my hand. Do you hear me?'

The water pipes rumbled as the bathroom taps were turned off.

'Get the fuck over here now, you stupid bitch.'

I heard a grunt and felt something hit my leg as he threw it. It stung but I didn't look down.

'Alice!' he snarled. 'Are you listening to me?'

I got to my feet and walked towards the door.

'Where the fuck are you going?'

A glass crashed into the wall beside me as I turned the handle and walked out into the hallway. I opened the door to the bathroom. Mum was sitting in the water and there was steam in the air.

'Why don't you let me do your back?' I said.

Kneeling down by the bath, I took the soap in my hand before plunging it into the water and rubbing it between my palms.

'We'll get you nice and clean, Mum,' I whispered.

I don't know why I defied The Idiot that day. I'd done it occasionally when I was younger and the kids were at home but had always given in after Mum or the kids were beaten even more to show me I couldn't say no for ever. But something changed that day. Maybe it was the realisation that I could never take the risk of another child being punished as Caitlin had been or maybe it was the fact that Michael had thrown me a lifeline by showing me there was finally somewhere I could run to. Or could it have been the fact that I had nothing left to lose? I had been beaten and raped since I was eleven years old but losing Caitlin meant nothing could ever hurt me again.

The next day, Dad turned on me as soon as we were alone together.

'Think you're going to get away with it, do you? Because you're not, you know. I'm going to slice up your mum and then you'll be sorry. Who the fuck do you think you are? You do as I say, when I say it, do you hear?'

I didn't answer back, look at him or even flinch when he walked up to me and stuck his face in mine. I didn't gasp when he threw something or slapped me. I didn't speak as he threw insults and I didn't jump to his orders as he told me to make him a cup of tea or get down to the shops. The Idiot got more and more enraged as the days went on and I stopped eating, drinking or even speaking.

'You've got to stop this, Alice,' Mum tried telling me. 'He's so angry with you. I don't know what he's going to do.'

But I didn't care any more. I wanted him to kill me, make good his promise once and for all so that I could be with Caitlin again. I just wanted him to do it – carry out the threats he'd been making all these years. Day after day I sat like a zombie, not moving or answering back, just waiting for him to finish me off. I'd seen my death a million times in my nightmares and now wanted him to finally kill me.

'You silly cow,' The Idiot screamed. 'You fat, useless slag. Can't have a baby, can't keep a baby, can't do anything but sit there like a lump.'

I just sat and waited. I knew that he'd snap eventually and for two long weeks I ignored him. I wouldn't speak to him or look at him or do anything he told me. Day after day The Idiot screamed and shouted but I didn't budge. I didn't care any more, I wanted him to pick up one of his knives and stab it into me, grab one of the guns and shoot me dead.

'This is fucking ridiculous,' he screamed one day when he got back from going to the shops with Mum to find me sitting in the same spot they'd left me in. 'It's going to stop, do you hear?'

His hand smashed into the side of my head.

'It's time you bucked up your ideas because otherwise I'll lock you up good and proper. There won't be any trips to the shops or TV. You'll be in that bedroom of yours for good. You won't move, breathe or sleep without my say-so.'

I got up silently and went into the bathroom. Sliding the lock across the door, I sat down on the toilet and stared into space. When was it going to end? When was he finally going to finish me?

'Alice!' he yelled outside the door. 'What are you doing in there?'

The door handle turned and I heard a shout.

'Open this door now,' he screamed.

I did nothing as he started kicking the door.

'Open up,' he shouted. 'Now!'

His foot repeatedly smashed into the door, kick after kick as he tried to break it down. I knew he'd be wild now; his hands would be itching to close around my throat. Dad howled with anger as his leg smashed into the door.

'Open up,' he shouted. 'Or I'll fucking kill you.'

The door gave way with a bang and I looked up. Dad stood in front of me, naked from the waist down and wearing nothing but an old grey T-shirt. He roared as he lunged at me and slapped me on the cheek.

'I'm going to fucking kill you if you don't buck up.'

I raised my head and looked at Dad for the first time in days.

Do it.

Kill me now.

Finish me off.

Let me be with Caitlin.

But as he stared at me, I saw something in his eyes that I'd never seen before – weakness and confusion. He knew what

I was trying to do and he wasn't going to let me. He was too scared. He was never going to kill me. I'd never be with Caitlin because he was too much of a coward to make good his threats.

I had to escape.

I couldn't wait for Mum any more. Dad was never going to kill me like he'd threatened to all these years. He was a bully, sadist and torturer but now I knew he was a coward too. I'd seen that and could never forget it. He'd never put me out of my misery. He'd keep me here for ever and I'd be alive in hell for the rest of my life.

CHAPTER TWENTY-TWO

Terror filled me as I got out of bed the next morning. I knew I had to leave soon or I would never find the courage again. I thought of Caitlin, the life she'd shown me, the life I might be able to have if only I got away from him. I'd packed a shopping trolley with a couple of pairs of jogging bottoms, a T-shirt and Caitlin's pictures. It was all I had to take with me apart from Michael's phone number which was stuffed in one of my socks. I'd got it the night before when I'd crept into the living room when Mum and Dad were asleep. I knew Mum had a book with phone numbers written in it and wanted to find Michael's. I'd never had his number but needed it because he was the only person who'd help me.

Holding my breath, I'd walked into the living room. We'd moved again and my new bedroom didn't open straight into the lounge like the last place. I had to get through two doors to get to the living room and I prayed they wouldn't squeak as I pulled them. It was almost pitch dark but I could make out the shapes of Mum and Dad lying on the bed. Someone was breathing heavily as I walked towards the sideboard near the door and felt around in the dark for the book. I found it and picked it up before turning around.

But just as I started creeping back to my room, a shape

shifted in the bed and the breathing stopped. I stood still and felt my legs shake beneath me. I was sure my heart was beating so loud it had woken someone up. It crashed in my ears as I waited for what seemed like for ever. When the snoring started again, I tiptoed back to my room where I copied down Michael's number on a piece of paper before getting back into bed.

Now my head raced as I got dressed and walked into the living room. I was ready but had no idea how I was going to get out of the flat. Dad kept the key with him at all times and only gave it to Mum and me if we had to go out. But the moment we got back, he'd shout for it and make sure we locked ourselves in again.

The Idiot was lying watching TV and Mum was sitting beside him as usual when I walked into the living room with a cup of tea. I drank it silently before standing up.

'I'll go and get your money then,' I said to him.

It was benefits day and I knew he'd want his cash as soon as possible.

'You're going out early,' he said. 'That's more like it.'

Mum unlocked the front door for me and I walked outside. There was no way I could run now because I had no money and couldn't leave the only things I had left of Caitlin. I felt so afraid. Being outside only reminded me of how big the world was, how endless it seemed. Would I be able to survive in it alone? I'd never had a job or lived a normal life. I'd been told what to eat, when to go to bed, when to speak and sleep. Fighting down panic, I walked to the post office and got Dad's money. I knew I couldn't take any because it would be stealing and I couldn't give him any ammunition to get help from the police to come after me. But tomorrow I'd have to go out and collect my own benefits. Maybe then I could take some money and run.

Mum let me in but turned towards the bathroom as I got over the threshold. Usually she locked up after me but today she was desperate for the toilet so I shut the door behind me. I walked into the living room as the phone rang and The Idiot picked it up. He didn't look at me as he talked to someone and I threw all his money on the bed except a twenty-pound note which I need to pay a bill. As soon as he'd checked everything was there, he'd send me back out again. He always had to make sure I hadn't kept a penny before sending me off to do errands.

Then suddenly I realised. The door was still unlocked. I had twenty pounds. This was my chance to escape. I had to do it now. In a blur, I walked out of the living room and pulled the door half closed before going into my bedroom to get the shopping trolley I'd packed. Tiptoeing back into the hall, I saw Mum standing waiting for me.

'I need to go,' I whispered. 'I have to go now, Mum.'

I didn't know how long I had before he stopped talking on the phone and realised something was wrong. I had to leave now. I didn't have time to think. I knew Mum wouldn't come with me. I'd asked a thousand times and she'd never agreed. She wouldn't do it now. She'd never leave him.

'I'm sorry, Mum, but I have to.'

'I know,' she said softly.

Mum started crying as I stared at her and for a moment I thought I wouldn't be able to leave. But then I remembered Caitlin. The life she'd shown me. The life I might still be able to have.

'I love you, Mum,' I said as I kissed her.

'I love you back,' she replied softly.

With a shaking hand, I opened the door and stepped outside. For a moment, I wanted to turn back. How would I ever do this? Be alone, without Mum and the only home I'd ever known. I forced myself to put one foot in front of another as I started walking down the road. I knew Mum would be watching me but I couldn't look back. I might run back to her if I did.

The skin on the back of my neck crawled as I walked down the road away from my prison. Would The Idiot see me from the window and come after me? Any minute now, I was sure I'd hear him scream my name just like he'd done for years.

I heard a shout and spun around. It was only some kids playing nearby and I hurried down the road with my head down. I knew he wouldn't run after me – he was too lazy for that – but he might get in the car and hunt me down. Almost breathless, I ran into a phone box outside a pub. There were cards with taxi numbers stuck all over the walls. My hand trembled as I lifted the phone and called one.

Hurry up. Hurry up.

Was he coming after me?

Would he find me and take me back?

The minutes dragged by as I stood waiting on the road. It seemed like for ever until a car eventually pulled up in front of me.

'You waiting for a taxi, love?' I heard a voice say. 'Are you Alice?'

A man was looking at me through the open car window.

'Yes,' I said, and reached for the door.

'Where to?' the man asked as I got into the car.

'The station.'

'Which one? There are loads in this city.'

'The main one.'

I didn't know where it was and I'd never seen it. But

maybe I would be able to get to Michael's from there and The Idiot would never think to look for me in a place like that. The taxi started moving and I stared out of the windows. I was sure he'd follow me. Maybe he was just behind us in his car. He was sure to come after me. He'd never let me go.

But there was no sign of him about twenty minutes later when the taxi pulled up outside a huge building.

'Here you are, love,' the driver said.

I paid him and got out of the car. I'd never been in a train station before. It was so busy and full of people rushing around as I stared up at the huge boards showing train information. How would I ever find the way to Michael's? I did not know how to get on a train or where to go. I jumped as I saw two police officers walking by. Were they looking for me? Had he told them I'd run away? I walked over to a phone box and bent down to get Michael's phone number hidden in my sock. I pulled it out before putting some money into the slot and dialling.

'Hello?' a voice said.

It was my brother.

'Hello?' he asked again.

I couldn't speak. Tears were running down my face. I was so scared. Why had I left Mum?

'Alice?' the voice said.

'Yes,' I gasped.

'Where are you?'

'At the station. I've run away. I've left him.'

'I know,' Michael said. 'He's been on the phone asking if you've called here and saying you'd gone.'

His voice sounded rough and angry. I almost wanted to put the phone down. Maybe Michael was angry I'd left.

'Have you got any money?' he said.

'A few pounds.'

'Well, get in a taxi to the bus station, get a cup of tea and wait for me. I'll come and find you.'

'Will you?'

'Of course. Just wait and I'll get you.'

I did as Michael said. Walking outside, I got into another taxi and asked to be taken to the bus station. It was just as busy – full of people carrying suitcases and running around. I saw the café and went in to get a cup of tea with the last of my money. If Michael didn't find me now then I had nothing. I felt light-headed and sick as I sat down. The café felt so crowded and noisy. Smoke in the air, lights flashing on signs, people chatting and bustling around. Would Michael find me? Or would Dad get to me first? I knew I couldn't go back now. I'd die if I did.

I felt a touch on my shoulder and whirled around. Michael was standing above me. I knew immediately that he wasn't angry with me – just scared and relieved I was safe. I jumped up and threw my arms around him, holding on to him so tight that he could hardly breathe.

'You're all right now, you're fine,' he said as he put his arms around me.

'But I've run away. He'll take me back.'

'No he won't, Alice.'

'He will. He won't let me go.'

'He has to. You've left now and I won't let him hurt you.'

CHAPTER TWENTY-THREE

I'd never known just how big the world was: shops full of clothes to pick and choose, cinemas with screens as big as houses and parks where green grass ran into the distance. In those first few weeks after I escaped, there were so many things to discover because all I'd ever really known were the few streets around whichever flat or house we'd lived in. I didn't have a clue about how much there was to see and do and it was almost overwhelming, as if the world had raced ahead and left me behind.

At first I kept close to Michael's home – too scared to go far for fear The Idiot was going to come after me. I knew he was furious that I'd left and had tried to cause trouble by calling the police. When two officers turned up at Michael's flat, I was sure they were there to take me back home. The Idiot had accused me of stealing from him but when I told them exactly what I had of his – a video card, an old rent book and some receipts – they advised me to just post them.

'But aren't you here to take me back?' I asked.

'No,' said one of the officers, looking at me strangely. 'You're an adult. Free to do what you like. Any argument with your father is nothing to do with us.'

Of course, The Idiot was furious that the police had

refused to do his dirty work for him and started phoning Michael to scream warnings about me: I was a slut, I'd be pregnant within a year to a junkie; I'd bring trouble to his door so Michael had better get rid of me. But even though he didn't come round to the flat and smash in the windows or load up a gun and come looking for me, I was still terrified because you can't wipe away years of fear in just a few days. I jumped every time the doorbell went and wanted to run when I heard the phone ring because although I was finally free, I was still waiting for The Idiot to take his revenge.

Michael and Julie didn't ask many questions as they looked after me and I didn't talk about what had happened. As far as they knew, I was a girl who'd lived with her parents too long because she wanted to look after her mother. All I said was that I'd had enough of putting up with The Idiot and Michael understood that. He knew, of course, that Mum and I had been hurt over the years because he hadn't forgotten what it was like to live with Dad. But both of us had let our secrets close up so tightly that no one wanted to drag them into the light and there was no way I'd ever tell Michael the whole truth because I was sure he'd go after Dad. For Julie and the girls' sake as well as his own, I couldn't risk seeing him end up in prison.

It wasn't just Michael that I wouldn't confide in, though. From the moment I left his home, I vowed to forget The Idiot. He'd taken too many years from me and I wouldn't give him any more. I knew I'd never tell anyone the whole truth about what had happened. I wanted to forget it and bury it deep inside me. It was as if it had happened to someone else in another life and for now I just wanted to start living. I still ached for Caitlin but told myself that this was the life she had shown me I could have and I had to live it for her.

The first thing Michael and Julie did was introduce me to all the family I'd never known. I knew several of Dad's family and had met Mum's nephew, Sam, and a few other relatives when we had lived with Michael in 1990. But now I met other relatives from Mum's side for the first time and there were so many of them – men and women with partners and kids – who piled into Michael and Julie's living room, opened bottles and started chatting. I don't think they were quite sure what to make of me at first because they couldn't understand why they'd never met me.

'I lived with my parents,' I explained.

'But why did you never come to visit Michael?'

'My mum was ill. I had to look after her.'

They didn't ask any more questions and I was glad they just accepted me into the group. To begin with, those nights seemed strange to me because I'd never done anything like that before and I sat quietly listening to everyone bantering with each other. I didn't understand their jokes. It didn't sound like fun to me as they took the micky out of each other and laughed. But I slowly learned this was what real families did because it showed affection. My new relatives were a bit rough and tough for sure but they were kind and fun. A family.

It wasn't the only new thing I was experiencing. From getting out of bed at whatever time I wanted, to deciding what to eat for my tea, each day was full of decisions I had never made before. I was twenty-seven and it scared me to be so free but Michael and Julie were very patient. The first few times I collected my benefit money, Julie took me to the shops and I blew every penny on clothes. I bought under-wear, trousers and tops, my first ever coat and even a pair of shoes with a little heel. I'd only ever worn trainers and felt so smart in my new shoes. I also couldn't believe all the cosmetics that were on sale. The Idiot hadn't even bought Mum and me toothpaste or sanitary towels half the time and now I had deodorant and perfume, moisturiser and even an anti-wrinkle cream.

I went to the pub and tried a glass of wine, visited a fast food restaurant and ordered a burger and went to see a children's film at the cinema – I'd only ever been once before when I was about fifteen and went with Michael. But the thing I loved most was looking after my nieces. I didn't know them that well when I first moved in because Julie had had a mother's intuition and never trusted Dad so she hadn't brought them to visit us much. But I soon got to know them and loved helping her look after the girls. It felt safe because it reminded me of the kids and Caitlin. I couldn't get enough of Paula and Jacqueline's happy, lively faces. In the mornings, I'd get up with them, sort out their breakfasts and walk them to school. Later on in the day, I'd pick them up and stop to let them play in the park on the way home without worrying about the clock. At weekends, we'd all go out together and do things. Each day with them amazed me.

But however much I tried to forget the past, I couldn't ignore it completely. I still thought a lot about Caitlin as I missed her desperately and couldn't stop wondering how Mum was. I knew I'd done what I had to do but felt so guilty about leaving her. When I closed my eyes I'd see her face as I said goodbye – she looked so sad and lost – and the day after arriving at Michael's, I sent a birthday card saying: 'Love you, miss you, see you soon.' I didn't know if she'd got it because I didn't hear anything from her. Maybe The Idiot had hurt her so badly she couldn't pick up the phone or maybe he was just being even more controlling now I'd gone. I tried calling her a few times but The Idiot always picked up the phone and hung up the moment he realised it was me. The only way I got any news of her was through Michael because when The Idiot finally stopped screaming abuse about me down the phone at him, my brother would ask after Mum.

'Maybe I should leave,' I said one day after another of Dad's phone calls. 'I don't want to make trouble for you and you know what he's like.'

'You're not going anywhere,' Michael told me. 'You're staying with us and that's final – no matter how much he moans about it.'

'But what if he comes here? What about Julie and the girls?'

'He won't. Trust me. You're safe.'

'Are you sure?'

'Yes. I'm a big boy now, Alice. I can handle him.'

'But you know what he's like.'

'Yes, I do and I know he won't show his face here. I've got too many friends who'd see to him.'

I told myself that Michael would know if anything terrible happened to Mum because he'd hear about it when Dad phoned. But I couldn't stop thinking of her and knew that if I wanted any kind of contact with Mum, I'd have to speak to or see The Idiot just as Michael had done for all these years. The thought terrified me but I knew I couldn't completely abandon Mum even though I'd left. She needed me and I still wanted to do whatever I could to help.

A few weeks after I ran away, I asked my cousin Sam to take me home to pick up some of my things. I was sure that as long as I was with someone, The Idiot would never try to hurt me. I'd seen what he was like over all those years – he only tortured me behind closed doors. But by the time

Sam and I got to the flat, I was trembling with fear as we knocked on the door and Mum opened it.

'Alice!' she exclaimed.

She looked so pale and drawn as I stepped forward to give her a hug.

'Hello, Mum,' I said, and put my arms around her.

But in that instant, The Idiot started shrieking. Hiding in the shadows of the flat, he must have heard Mum say my name.

'Shut the fucking door,' he barked. 'Get her out of here otherwise I'll come after her myself. She's made her choice and now she's dead to us.'

Without a word, Mum pulled away from me.

'Please,' I cried. 'Just a minute.'

But the door slammed shut and, as I stared at it, I wondered how I'd ever get to see Mum again. A few weeks later Michael found out she was in hospital and we both knew The Idiot would only take it out on her if I went to visit. Michael tried but got turned away because Dad had instructed that no one was to see Mum. It was just as I'd feared: The Idiot might have lost me but he was still going to punish Mum to get back at me. I had no idea when or if I'd see her again. Mum had been everything to me for so long, the reason I'd stayed for all those years, and it felt like I'd lost my best friend now she wasn't with me.

Three months after I left home, I moved out of Michael's flat. I'd just turned twenty-eight and felt scared of going it alone but knew it was time to start relying on myself. I'd spent so long being controlled that I had to learn how to live my own life now. Michael arranged for me to move in with one of my new relatives in a flat up the road from my cousin Sam because he wanted people around to keep an eye on me. I decided that I'd let myself settle in to my new home before finding out about things like going to college and taking some exams or finding a job and working like Michael. There were so many possibilities which had opened up to me now I was free.

Free.

I kept saying the word in my head because I could hardly believe it. After all those years, I was finally rid of The Idiot and each morning when I woke up in my new room, I reminded myself how lucky I was. Michael had painted the bedroom for me and put down a laminate floor. It was so clean and new – all mine – and now I had the beginnings of a real life including a place to live and some friends.

After moving into the flat, I saw a lot of Sam and his girl-friend. I'd grown close to them and enjoyed spending the evening at their flat watching TV. They had loads of friends and, although I still kept myself to myself a lot, there was one in particular who caught my attention. He was called Steven and I met him when Sam invited me over to have a drink to celebrate my new home.

At first I thought Steven was a bit annoying, to be honest. Always making jokes and bumping his leg into mine as we sat on the sofa, he was five years younger than me and seemed so cocky. But when I got up to leave at the end of the night, he offered to see me safely home and as we got to my front door, it was obvious that he had other ideas when I turned to say goodnight.

'Can I have a cup of tea?' he asked cheekily.

'All right then, but just a quick one,' I replied as I walked into the flat.

And then the strangest thing happened, something that I didn't expect at all. Steven kissed me as we stood in the hallway and suddenly I felt tingly, excited and scared all at the same time. When I pulled away from him, he followed me into the living room and sat down on the sofa beside me.

'I'd like to kiss you again,' he said.

'Why?'

'Because I like you, Alice,' he replied with a laugh.

My head was rushing as he bent towards me. I couldn't believe this was happening. I was in my own flat, able to do whatever I wanted and for the first time in my life I could let a man kiss me without knowing I'd be beaten for it later on. So when Steven asked if he could spend the night, I said yes. I knew it was too quick, I knew I wasn't ready and felt scared as we lay down together. But more than anything I wanted to know what it was like to feel normal – I'd spent so long dreaming of it and now was my chance to find out.

Of course, when I woke up in the morning I couldn't believe what I'd done and felt scared all over again. But Steven kept coming back to see me even though I'd told him I wouldn't sleep with him again. After all the years of being told by The Idiot that men were after just one thing, I was sure he would soon lose interest. But Steven seemed happy to be my friend because he talked to me and showed an interest in my life; when he held my hand, he didn't pressurise me.

I was still convinced, though, that one day he'd want to take things further again and it terrified me because the night we'd spent together had shown me I'd never be like normal women. I'd frozen when Steven had touched me in a certain way or turned away when he'd used familiar words and memories of The Idiot had run through my head. Steven, though, didn't know what was hidden inside me and continued to phone and visit. After going away for a week, he arrived back to tell me how much he'd missed me and I felt wanted for the first time in my life. As the weeks passed and we got to know each other better, I felt comfortable enough to sleep with him again and soon we were in a relationship together.

I almost couldn't believe what had happened: in just a few months I'd got a boyfriend and a flat – the kind of things most people take for granted but to me were more precious than I could ever have imagined. But however kind and gentle Steven was, I didn't relax physically with him and, although I tried to explain a little about my past, I couldn't tell him everything. All I said was that my dad had been violent and not looked after his kids well. I just wanted Steven to have some idea about what had happened to me so that he might understand that it wasn't him who made me freeze in bed but my memories.

'Let's just take it easy, day by day,' Steven told me when I sobbed out a tiny bit of the truth of my past.

He was as good as his word: patient and tender, reassuring and kind, and slowly I started to relax. We went out for walks or to the shops, visited friends and relatives together just like other couples I saw around me. It felt as if my life was finally beginning.

But then something happened which changed everything. It was a couple of months after meeting Steven when I made myself a cup of coffee one morning and was violently sick afterwards. I didn't think much about it – just as I didn't realise my period was late. After all the years of counting down the days and hours each month with Dad, I enjoyed not living in fear now. But when a couple of weeks went by and my period still didn't arrive, I knew I couldn't ignore what was happening any more and went to the doctor. When she confirmed what I already knew, I felt scared but almost excited as well.

Maybe deep down, I'd wanted to get pregnant to prove that I could have the family I'd dreamed of; maybe I'd taken chances with Steven because part of me was sure I would never have another baby; maybe I just wanted to be like other women. I'm not sure how it happened but the moment I heard those words, I knew I'd have the baby. I'd love this child and give it the life that Caitlin hadn't had. Besides, how could I get rid of a baby whose father I was falling in love with?

Whatever my feelings though, I was sure that Steven wouldn't be able to handle the news. We'd only just met each other, it was all so new and he was only twenty-three – too young to handle such a big responsibility. I'd have to do this alone but I was determined to because I wanted to make something of my life and what better way was there of doing that than having a baby?

'I understand if you don't want to be a dad,' I told Steven that night as we sat in my bedroom. 'I know it's all too fast and unexpected. Please don't feel as if you have to stay with me, because you don't.'

'What do you mean?' Steven asked.

'I mean I'm going to have this baby but I'll do it alone if I have to.'

I looked down at my hands lying in my lap. I might have sounded brave but how would I cope with a baby when I was only just learning to live an adult life myself?

'You're not going to do this alone, Alice,' Steven said.

I felt his arm around my shoulders as he pulled me to him.

'I want you and I want our baby.'

'You do?'

'Yes.'

'But we've only known each other a couple of months. How will we manage?'

'We'll be fine. I want to be with you both.'

'You do?'

'Of course.'

'But why?'

'Isn't it obvious?' Steven said with a laugh as he hugged me. 'Because I love you, Alice.'

CHAPTER TWENTY-FOUR

A year after I ran away, I moved into a new home with Steven. The baby was due in a couple of months and sometimes I almost had to pinch myself. How could I be this happy?

'Will it be a boy or a girl?' Steven would ask as he stroked my huge tummy.

'I don't mind as long as our baby's healthy,' I'd reply.

When Steven hugged me to him, I felt safer than I ever had in my life. He'd got a job as a kitchen porter so we had a bit of money coming in, we were living in a lovely flat and I was going to be a mother. It was all I'd ever wanted and I felt happier than I'd ever imagined I could be. Just tiny ordinary things like cooking and cleaning or sitting with Steven chatting about the future and trying to guess what the baby would look like excited me.

Friends and relatives had been surprised by our news but were happy for us when they realised that Steven and I were going to stick together. They'd all rallied round to help and Steven had decorated our new flat with Michael and my cousin Sam. The other person who'd helped out was my brother Simon, who'd arrived on my doorstep more than ten years after running away from The Idiot. Simon had found me easily because the area I lived in was small and everyone knew everyone else. But I still couldn't believe it when he turned up and I opened the door to see him.

'Alice?' he'd said as he stood on the doorstep, and I knew immediately that it was my younger brother.

I could hardly speak as I looked at Simon. I had thought so much about all the kids for so many years and now one of them was standing in front of me.

I was so happy and knew Mum would be too. We'd never spoken much about the kids in the years after they left but I knew she thought about them a lot. Simon was twenty-seven now and I'd often wondered where he was – just as I'd thought about where all my brothers and sisters had ended up and what kind of lives they'd had. We'd had the odd letter through the years: Laura had been in care for four years before leaving – moving from a children's home to a foster family; Kate had been fostered ever since she was a little girl by the same family who'd wanted to adopt her while Charlie had been moved between foster carers and children's homes. But it had been years since we'd had any real news and I was overwhelmed when Simon arrived back in my life.

It was bittersweet, though, because he felt like a stranger to me now that so many years had passed and he wasn't the little brother I remembered any more. Slowly I discovered how hard his life had been – moving from home to home and never finding anywhere to settle. Simon had had a lot of health problems and, although he didn't say it himself, it was obvious that he'd had as much trouble laying the past to rest as I had.

'Let's not go into all that,' Simon would say if we came close to talking about it. 'It was all long ago and I don't want to know any more than I do.'

I respected his feelings and didn't force him to talk about things. I felt the same way as he did and was glad Simon wasn't dragging up the past. I was just happy to do whatever I could for my brother and told him he could stay with us for as long as he liked.

The one person I knew was spitting about my pregnancy was The Idiot. I hadn't been able to keep it a secret from him however much I wanted to because Michael had told Mum. I knew Dad had predicted all along that I would get pregnant quickly and it upset me to think of him sneering about how right he'd been. But I told myself Steven and I would prove him wrong because this wasn't just a flash in the pan whatever insults my father threw at us. Mum was happy and that was all that mattered to me. I'd seen her a couple of times in the year since The Idiot had made her slam the door in my face and the first occasion was not long after I'd moved out of Michael's when Mum was admitted to hospital again.

'I've got to go and see her,' I said to Michael when he told me. 'Dad won't be looking after her properly. She won't have clean clothes or underwear. She needs me to see to that for her.'

'He won't let you,' my brother replied. 'He's already told me to tell you that you're to stay away because you're not wanted.'

My blood boiled when I heard the message from Dad. What right had he to try to push me around even now? Who was he to tell me what to do? I couldn't stop thinking about it until one afternoon a few days later when I was at Michael's flat having a cup of tea with Julie and looked out of the window to see Dad's car outside. Michael was standing by the car talking to him.

Without a word, I left the flat and walked downstairs. I'd known ever since running away that this day would come.

I couldn't disappear and never see him again; there was Mum to think of and Michael was still in contact with him. However much I hated The Idiot, I was going to have to keep his secrets even now I was free and I was prepared to do it as long as he left me alone and let me see Mum now and again.

But still my stomach flipped as I walked outside and saw Dad's familiar figure hunched in the front seat. Taking a deep breath, I walked up to the window and knocked on the glass. The Idiot's eyes were pure hate as he opened the window and I took another deep breath as he looked at me. I wouldn't let him see that I was scared of him any more. I'd bury it so deep that he wouldn't know and have power over me again. I was stronger now; I'd defied him and run away, I was building a new life.

'I'd like to take some things up to Mum,' I said as he looked at me. 'She'll need a few bits and I want to see her.'

My stomach churned as I spoke and I wished my heart would stop hammering.

'Get the fuck out of my sight,' The Idiot spat as he stared ahead. 'She doesn't want to see you.'

'I'm sure she does.'

'No, she doesn't. Don't you get it, you stupid bitch? You're not her daughter any more. You're nothing to us.'

'But you can't tell me what to do!' I screamed.

My bravery dissolved the moment I saw The Idiot's black eyes boring into me – daring me to answer back again. Suddenly I felt like a little girl. It was as if I was in the living room when I was six years old, watching him scream at me and wondering when he'd hurt me, how quickly I'd have to move to dodge his fists.

'What?' he spat. 'Shut the fuck up and get away from me.'

Michael stepped forward.

'Come on, Dad. Why don't you let Alice take a few things up?'

'Because she's nothing to do with us now.'

Without another word, Dad wound up the window as I stood shaking on the pavement. Why couldn't I stand up to him even now? I'd felt so much braver since leaving home but the moment I saw him, I was as terrified as I ever had been. When would I grow up and stop being scared?

As Dad drove the car away, I told myself that The Idiot wasn't going to stop me this time. I might not be able to stand up to him face to face but I was going to see Mum whether he liked it or not. That night, I waited until visiting hours were over before going up to the hospital and sneaking on to the ward where Mum was being treated. The nurses kindly agreed to let me in as long as I was quick. Mum's blood pressure was far too high again and she'd had a bad angina attack so she needed a lot of rest.

'Mum?' I whispered as I stood by her bed.

I touched her hand gently. She was sleeping propped up on pillows and didn't answer. There was a bruise on her cheek.

'Mum?' I said a little more loudly, and she opened her eyes.

'Alice?'

'Yes, Mum, it's me.'

I sat down beside her and took her hand in mine.

'I've come to see you. I wanted to know how you were.'

'So-so,' she said as she smiled. 'How did you find out I was here?'

'Michael told me. I wasn't allowed to come but I had to.'

I was so happy to see her. I'd missed her so much. Guilt poured into me as I saw how sick she looked.

'Let's get you cleaned up and changed,' I said.

A nurse helped me draw the curtains about the bed and I gently took off the hospital gown Mum was wearing. She was very breathless as I undressed her and I had to go slowly so as not to tire her out. But eventually we got her into a clean nightshirt and dressing gown before propping her back up on the pillows again.

'Thanks, love,' she said as she lay back down.

I stared at the bruise on her face.

'Has he been hurting you?'

'No.'

She didn't look at me when she said it and I didn't believe her. But we didn't talk about it any more, just as we didn't talk about the fact that I'd run away. Mum and I were used to keeping silent about things and I think we were both so pleased to see each other that nothing else mattered. For the next week while she was in hospital, I saw her every day – going in at the end of visiting hours to avoid bumping into Dad, which meant I could never stay long but was enough time to check she had everything she needed and talk to her a little.

'How are things?' I asked towards the end of the week.

We both knew she'd soon be going home again and that meant I wouldn't be able to see her.

'The same,' she said.

When Mum was finally discharged from hospital, I knew she'd be running around for The Idiot the moment she got home. He was slowly killing her and there was nothing I could do to stop it. I longed for her to do what I had done but knew I couldn't push her. She had to decide for herself.

The next time I saw Mum was after I'd found out I was pregnant and I took Steven with me when she was admitted to hospital again.

'Look after her,' Mum told him as we sat and chatted. 'She's so precious to me.'

'I will,' Steven replied.

I was all alone in the flat when I heard the doorbell ring and opened the door. He was standing waiting for me.

'You knew I'd be back, didn't you?' The Idiot hissed.

I couldn't move. There was no one with me. Steven was out. Dad pushed his way past me into the flat. The moment the door was closed, he started screaming.

'Who the fuck do you think you are? You should have known better after all this time. Did you think I'd give up that easy?'

My throat was tight with fear; I couldn't breathe as he stood in front of me. I could smell his bitter skin, see the spit cracked and dry in the corners of his mouth.

'Cat got your tongue, then?' he laughed. 'Look at you – as fat as ever, useless little slag. Get in the bedroom.'

I didn't move.

'Now,' he roared.

I knew I had to do as he said, just like always.

Without a word, I walked towards the bedroom and opened the door. My hands closed around my huge tummy as I felt him behind me, his breath on my neck as he pushed me towards the bed. I gasped as his hands closed around my neck. I knew what he wanted. I couldn't get away. I'd never get away . . .

I opened my eyes.

I was lying in bed beside Steven and the grey half-light of early morning was coming in through the curtains. I could feel my face wet with tears and my heart thumping inside me.

'Sssh,' Steven said as he put his arms around me. 'You're okay. I'm here.'

'I need a drink,' I said as I pushed him away and got up out of bed.

I shut the bedroom door as I felt the tears rushing up inside me. Gasping for air, I walked into the bathroom and splashed my face with water before going into the living room and sitting down. I felt sick as I started crying and wrapped my hands around my belly. The dreams were like this all the time now. I couldn't seem to stop them no matter how many times I told myself during the day that I had to forget. My mind just wouldn't let me when I fell asleep and it all opened up inside me again. The Idiot was as real to me then as flesh and blood.

'You're safe at home,' I said silently to myself over and over. 'He won't come here. He can't touch you any more.'

I got up and went to get a photo album I kept in a drawer. Turning the pages, I stared at the few pictures I had of Caitlin and tried to remember the happy times with her. But other pictures kept filling my mind: Dad's face twisted in rage, his fists being raised – just like in my dreams. There was one I had often in which I saw Mum and me trapped in a room together while he lashed out at us until we were bleeding and cut.

'There's an improvement,' he'd sneer as Mum and I cowered in a corner.

I felt so afraid even when I woke up and pushed Steven away as he tried to comfort me. I didn't want to tell him about my dreams or let my old life spill into the new. I wanted to try to keep them apart, not let one contaminate the other. But ever since I'd left home, I'd had these dreams and now they were getting worse. I was going to have our baby soon and kept telling myself that things would change when I did. It would be a new life and I'd be happy. I knew I would be because I could still remember how I'd felt about Caitlin. If only the dreams would go away.

'Alice?'

Steven was standing in the door as I sat holding Caitlin's picture with tears running down my face.

'What is it?' he asked.

I could not speak. He walked towards me.

'I know you miss her but we've got a new life now,' Steven said. 'Caitlin's looking down on her new baby brother or sister about to be born.'

I stared at him as my secrets tore up inside me. I couldn't bear it any more. I couldn't hold them in any longer. I wanted to tell him that The Idiot was still ruining my life even though I'd escaped him.

'Are you coming back to bed?' Steven asked.

I had to do it. I had to tell him now. I couldn't keep silent any more. But how would he ever understand? Steven was just a young man. He came from a decent family and had never seen the things I had. I wanted him to look at me as he always had done. In his eyes I was Alice, his Alice. But if I told him, I was scared he'd never see me in the same way again. He'd think I was damaged goods, just as Dad had always said men would. Steven didn't have a clue about a life like mine. No one did. I'd never told anyone my secrets about Jonathan and Caitlin, the babies I'd been forced to carry.

'What's the matter, Alice?' Steven asked. 'Please tell me what's wrong. I know something's not right.'

'Caitlin was such a beautiful baby,' I whispered.

'I know, Alice, and soon we'll have our own but you'll never forget her.'

I stared at the picture.

'She was so beautiful considering what she was born into.'

Steven walked towards me.

'What do you mean? What was Caitlin born into?'

He'd been asking me more and more about The Idiot lately and why I wasn't allowed to see Mum. I knew he could sense that something was terribly wrong even though he didn't know what it was.

'She couldn't help who her dad was,' I said softly.

'What are you saying, Alice? Who was Caitlin's dad?'

I took a deep breath. I had to speak out. I had to say the words I'd kept inside for so many years.

'My father,' I whispered.

Steven's face clouded over as he struggled to understand what I meant.

'My father hurt me,' I sobbed. 'I was eleven when it started. I was just a girl. He made me do it otherwise he'd hurt Mum and my brothers and sisters.'

'You mean he touched you?'

'Yes.'

'But you were a child then. You had Caitlin when you were twenty-six.'

'I know.'

Steven said nothing. Then suddenly I saw rage burn into his eyes as my words sunk in.

'Please don't be angry with me,' I pleaded. 'I wasn't sure I should tell you.'

'Of course you should!' he shouted. 'But why didn't you before? Why did it take you this long? That fucking bastard.'

'I've never told anyone,' I sobbed.

'But why not? Why didn't you ask for help?'

I looked up at Steven.

'Because he told me he'd kill me if I did and he had the guns and knives to do it. I'm so sorry, Steven. But I couldn't keep any more secrets with the baby coming.'

I felt sick inside. I'd finally told someone the truth. What

The Idiot had done was no longer a secret shared by just him and me.

'Tell me you don't hate me,' I cried as Steven sat next to me. 'Please say you still want me and the baby.'

'Of course I do, Alice. I hate him and what he did to you but nothing can break us up now.'

I held on to Steven as tightly as I could and sobbed. I couldn't believe I had told someone the truth at last. All I could hope now was that the dreams would finally be over.

CHAPTER TWENTY-FIVE

'It's a girl,' the midwife said, and I grabbed Steven's hand.

For a few awful seconds, the room was quiet and I thought of Jonathan and Caitlin and how silent they'd been. But then there was a wail and my daughter was lifted on to my chest for the first time.

'She's beautiful,' Steven exclaimed, and I stared at my baby, hardly daring to believe she was real.

Emma was born by caesarean in spring 1999 and she was a chubby baby with a puff of hair. Steven looked fit to burst as I passed her to him and a smile stretched across his face. I saw pure love in his eyes as I watched him.

I couldn't wait to get home and was glad when I was discharged three days later and we climbed into a taxi carrying Emma in a car seat. As the doors closed, it suddenly felt strange to be leaving the safety of the hospital. From now on this tiny baby would be ours to feed and clothe, love and keep safe. But then Steven looked at me, we looked down at Emma and I knew everything would be all right.

I soon got into a routine with the baby. Steven was out all day at work so I'd feed and change her, take her for walks and go to see friends. Emma was amazing, intoxicating almost, and I breathed in her smell every chance I got. It was so pure and clean that I couldn't get enough of it. I also couldn't stop cuddling her and, even though I knew I wasn't supposed to, I let her fall asleep on me because I couldn't resist the feeling of having her tiny body resting softly against mine.

My favourite times were just after Emma was born when the world seemed to close in on us and everything was quiet. She would fall asleep on me as Steven sat next to us and it felt as if we were in a bubble nothing could ever break into. The only time I drew the line and got bossy was when Steven wanted Emma in bed to sleep with us.

'No!' I exclaimed. 'What if I roll on her and hurt her? We can have a cuddle but then she's to go into her cot.'

She was such a hungry baby and I loved breastfeeding, something I'd never been able to do with Caitlin. I often thought about her as the weeks turned into months and Emma grew. It was only now that I realised just how different Caitlin had been to other babies as I learned something new every day with Emma: her first smile or being able to hold her head up, rolling over or gurgling at me.

A few weeks after we got home, Mum phoned to say she wanted to see Emma. I agreed to let her visit because it would mean so much to her, even though I knew she'd have to bring The Idiot. I didn't want to have Dad in my home but would allow it for her sake. I owed Mum that much and because I hoped that some day The Idiot might let me see her more regularly, I couldn't cross him. Mum and Dad were a package and I had to put up with him to see her.

Not everyone felt the same way though. After I'd confessed about the past to Steven, he'd wanted me to go to the police and even though I'd eventually convinced him my silence was the best thing for us all, I knew he was unhappy. My brother Simon, who was still staying with us, hadn't laid eyes on Dad since the day he was driven out of home years ago and couldn't stop himself flying at The Idiot when he walked into the flat with Mum. Grabbing Dad by the throat, Simon pinned him to the wall as years of pain and anger exploded inside him.

'I'm going to kill you,' he screamed.

Simon's face was wild, his eyes burning as he strangled Dad. The Idiot tried to push Simon away but he was too strong for him now. The little boy he'd beaten and cursed was a man and The Idiot's eyes were wide as he struggled. I rushed towards the two men. It was just as it had been when we were children but this time it was Dad's turn to be bullied and, however much I didn't want to rescue him, I couldn't allow Simon to do this in my home with Emma nearby.

'Go on then, you little bastard,' The Idiot howled. 'You haven't got the fucking bottle.'

My brother's mouth twisted in pain as he stared at The Idiot.

'No, Simon!' I shouted. 'Not here. This is my home.'

My brother looked at me and I saw his hands fall from around Dad's throat. Without a word, he stepped back and walked away.

'We're going,' The Idiot snarled. 'Now!'

Mum left without seeing Emma and phoned to say Dad wouldn't bring her back as long as Simon was staying with me. I knew I would have to take the baby to see Mum however much I hated going back to the flat. Now I had a home of my own, I could finally see how squalid and filthy it really was and there was no way I was going to risk Emma picking up anything in the mess so I refused to get her out of the car seat while we were there and just passed her quickly to Mum for a cuddle before putting her back safely under her blanket.

The Idiot looked angry the whole time I was there and I was glad to leave because I still felt scared being anywhere near him. But I was also happy that Mum had seen her granddaughter because I knew it meant a lot to her. After that day, I started to visit every now and again and it was as if an uneasy truce sprung up between The Idiot and me: we did not speak or look at each other and I made sure there was always someone with us in the room. Just as we had done for so many years, my family did not mention the past or the fact that I had run away. The present closed over whatever had gone before and people accepted things because it was easier than asking questions.

Steven, though, struggled to understand how I could even go near Dad.

'He's an animal,' he'd say. 'He should be locked up for what he did.'

I tried my best to explain that if I didn't put up with Dad then I'd never see Mum again and, if I suddenly stopped seeing her, Michael would start asking questions and I didn't want to risk having the past raked up once more. I wanted it left where it was, behind me, and didn't even discuss it with Steven after the night I told him.

But sometimes he'd look at me in confusion and start asking questions I didn't want to answer. I was happy now and didn't want to ruin things with terrible memories. I knew it was hard for him to understand because he hadn't had a life like mine but in the end Steven agreed to let me visit Mum as long as I didn't go too often. I promised him that Dad would never touch a hair on Emma's head. For all those years when I was his prisoner, I'd been isolated and weak but now I had friends and family – a whole network of

people who would make The Idiot pay if he touched my
daughter and he knew that. I might have kept quiet about
what Dad had done to me but it didn't need to be said
that I'd scream it from the rooftops if he hurt Emma.

I also think Steven accepted my visits because, however
much he didn't like them, he knew Mum and I were joined
by a bond that nothing could rip apart. I had a new life
now but could never forget her. Even all those years on
from losing the kids to social services, I still felt guilty
about what it had done to Mum and the part I'd played. I
was also sure I'd be punished if I let her down again – just
as I had been when I'd failed Jonathan and Caitlin.

As I watched Emma grow and flourish, I'd never felt
happier. I was in control of my life, things were good and
Steven seemed as happy as I was. Even so, I had no idea just
how much life was going to change one night as we sat on the
sofa watching TV. Emma was a couple of months old and
Steven had been a bit distracted for a few days but I hadn't
asked him about it because I knew he'd tell me when he was
ready. Maybe being a dad was scaring him a little. It shouldn't
have done, though. He was great with Emma and helped out
as much as possible when he came home from work.

But on this night he just couldn't get settled – getting up
and leaving the room before coming back in, sitting down
again and starting to fidget next to me. Then he'd stare at
me and take a deep breath before turning away.

'What's wrong?' I asked.

'I just need the toilet.'

'Well go then!' I said with a laugh.

He went out again, came back two minutes later and sat
down.

'Shall I make us a cup of tea?' I asked, and started to get
up off the sofa.

'Don't go!' Steven exclaimed.

I watched in shock as he jumped off the couch and knelt on the floor.

'What are you doing?' I gasped.

'There's something I want to ask.'

I couldn't speak as he dug into his jeans pocket and pulled out a box. Opening it, he showed me a ring with a tiny stone in it.

'Will you marry me, Alice?' Steven asked. 'I love you and Emma and I want us to be together always.'

I looked at him, hardly daring to believe this was happening.

'Please, Alice,' Steven said.

'Yes,' I whispered as I threw my arms around him.

For so long, I could never have believed I'd be this happy.

Steven and I decided that we wouldn't have a big wedding. We wanted to get married as soon as possible with no fuss because after all the years of being hidden away, I still didn't like being around lots of people and knew I wouldn't enjoy a big reception. Besides, we didn't have enough money for more than a few sausage rolls so a small wedding would suit us. I was happy for it to be Steven, Emma and my cousin Sam, who was going to be the best man. The only other person I wanted there was Mum, whom I'd asked to be my matron of honour.

'I wouldn't miss it for the world,' she told me, and I wondered what she'd have to do to persuade Dad to let her come to the wedding.

Somehow she did but I was still worried because Dad was going to drive Mum up to the registry office and I couldn't bear the thought of him seeing me marry. Steven told me he'd deal with it, though, and while I didn't know how he was going to get The Idiot out of the way, I hoped he would. I wanted it to be our special day and that meant not having Dad anywhere near me when I said my vows.

After booking a slot at the local registry office, I went shopping for something to wear. No one knew about the wedding – not even Michael. He'd fallen out with Steven over something stupid and I was worried he'd think I was making a mistake so I'd decided not to tell him. Maybe I was being selfish but I didn't want anything to burst the bubble of happiness around me.

But a few days before the wedding, my brother phoned.

'Is there something you want to tell me?' he asked, sounding a bit angry.

'No.'

'Are you sure, Alice?'

'Yes, of course.'

'Well, that's not what I've heard. Dad's told me you're getting married.'

I should have known he'd try to stir up an argument any which way he could.

'I'm sorry, Michael,' I said. 'It's just that things are a bit difficult between you and Steven. I don't want a big fuss made anyway.'

'But you're getting married, Alice, and what I think doesn't matter. It's your life and it's time you made your own decisions.'

I immediately felt guilty because I should have known that Michael would be happy for me.

'Anyway, I know what I'm going to give you as a wedding present,' he said.

'Don't be daft,' I exclaimed. 'You don't need to get us anything.'

'But I want to. I'm going to do you a buffet after the ceremony. We've got to celebrate a little.'

'Are you sure? It will be so much trouble.'

'Come on, sis. I want to do it. You'll be surprised at how good I've got at cooking.'

Michael had worked in hotel kitchens so I knew he'd do me proud but I wasn't sure if I wanted a party. It meant even more people would know about the wedding and I felt nervous about the attention. But I agreed to his plan because I didn't want to upset him again and Steven was pleased.

By the time the day arrived, I was almost beside myself with nerves. Steven was at home and I was at my cousin Sam's house where his girlfriend was helping me get ready in the cream dress I'd bought to wear. Emma was wearing a beautiful flowery dress with a matching hat and I was going to leave her to be looked after by Michael and Julie during the ceremony. I waited nervously until the doorbell rang which told me that Dad had arrived in the car with Mum to pick me up.

'It'll never last,' he sneered as I opened the door.

I knew exactly what he'd been saying to anyone who'd listen: I was a stupid fool, desperate, my marriage was a joke because I'd mess it up within months.

'Hi, Mum,' I said as I got into the car. 'You look lovely.'

I'd never seen Mum looking so smart. She was wearing a pale blue dress and jacket and I fixed my eyes on the back of her head as we drove to the registry office. I had to block Dad out of my mind. I wanted Mum to be here so I just had to find a way to ignore that he was even with us. But the journey to the registry office seemed to go on for ever. Would The Idiot deliberately try to make us late or even stop me from getting to the registry office at all? Was he determined to ruin this day for me? As I sat in the back of the car, I prayed Steven would be as good as his word. I didn't know how he was going to get Dad out of the way but I knew he had to. This was one thing The Idiot wasn't going to take from me, one hour of one day that I didn't want him to be part of.

We walked into the foyer of the registry office to find Steven and Sam waiting for us. They smiled as a woman came towards us.

'Are you ready?' she asked as she pointed to our left. 'I'm going to take you into that room over there where we'll conduct the ceremony.'

She turned to Dad.

'Only four people are allowed in,' she said. 'If you'd like to wait here that would be fine.'

The Idiot's face was like thunder as we started to walk away. He looked fit to murder someone then and there. But he couldn't say a word as the door closed and Mum took my hand.

'I told you I wouldn't let you down,' she whispered, and we smiled at each other.

Happiness bubbled up inside me. Mum's eyes were bright. We'd shown him. I couldn't believe Steven had done as he'd promised – kept me safe on the most important day of my life. I felt so brave and excited.

'Thank you,' I whispered to him as we stood beside each other.

When the ceremony was over, The Idiot pushed his way into the room to see the signing of the register but I didn't care. I had got married without him and after we'd written out our names, I kissed Steven as we walked towards the door where Sam was standing with his camcorder to take a film of us. I wanted to laugh as I looked at Dad's face. He looked ready to burst a blood vessel.

After today, I felt brave enough for anything. Dad had

always told me this day would never come and now it had. I was going to prove him wrong. I knew a man could be tender and talk to a woman without hurting her; that I could have happiness and maybe I wasn't as bad as he'd always made me believe. I'd show him that I could be married and happy just like other women. I didn't need to intimidate people or terrorise them like he did to have a family. Steven, Emma and I were together and I'd show him that I could make it work.

Later we arrived at Michael's flat and it took my breath away. Laid out on the table were huge bowls of food and bottles of wine and cans of beer. Party poppers banged as we walked into the living room to see Michael, Julie, the girls, Simon, Sam and some of my other cousins and their partners.

'Congratulations!' they all shrieked.

'I can't believe you've done all this,' I said as Michael hugged me.

'Why not? I used to do it when we were kids, didn't I?'

We had a brilliant night – laughing, chatting and singing together while The Idiot sat glowering in a corner. When I finally got home with Steven and we put Emma down to sleep, I sat and reran the day in my mind. It had been perfect, just as I'd always dreamed it would be: the best day of my life.

Three months later I fell pregnant again. Steven and I were going to have another baby. We were a proper family now and I could almost believe that I'd finally left the past behind me. But soon I would learn that however much I tried to outrun my memories, they would always catch up with me in the end.

CHAPTER TWENTY-SIX

I think those first couple of years after I escaped were like the first few seconds when you fall over – you know you're hurt but can't feel it yet. For two years, Steven and I were really happy but by the time our second daughter Lily was born, the cracks had started to appear. I thought burying the past would make it go away but I was wrong. As time went on, my nightmares started to return and I pushed Steven away as the memories overwhelmed me. Sometimes, I'd wake up and swear I could smell The Idiot on my skin or hear his voice taunting me. Even during the day, I couldn't forget the worthlessness he'd drilled into me as it crept back inside.

Maybe Steven was too young to cope with the responsibilities of a family or maybe when I told him who I really was he didn't want me any more. I don't know what had made things fall apart so quickly but as soon as we got married and real life started, it was as if we did not know each other any more. I felt completely rejected and developed severe post-natal depression after Lily's birth in 2000. I'd sit for hours staring into space or crying endlessly as I remembered the past. The guilt I had pushed down for so many years about my miscarriages, Jonathan and Caitlin flooded over me. Now I had two children, I felt even more of a monster. Vivid memories filled me and Dad's words rang in my head as I wondered if I could do anything right. I felt as if I could hardly cope with Lily and Emma – they never stopped needing something from me and I was drained of all energy and strength. I loved them, of course, but how could I be a good mum when I was such a bad person?

If I wasn't the woman Steven thought he'd married, though, he wasn't the man I believed he was either. As things between us got worse, he spent more and more time out with friends and sometimes our fights were vicious when he finally got home. The happy and kind man I had fallen in love with had disappeared and although I didn't completely understand what had driven him away, I was sure it was my fault. I knew I should never have told him about my past because Steven found it even more difficult to forget than I did. Always, we came back to the same argument: why did I stay so long? Why didn't I run away years before? I hardly knew what the answers were myself, and the more Steven asked me about it, the guiltier I felt. Maybe Dad was right, maybe I was as weak and stupid as he had always told me, if even the man I'd loved and trusted couldn't understand.

The questions Steven asked cut into my heart because they were the same ones I asked myself.

'Why did you stay?' he'd ask repeatedly. 'Everyone has a choice in life.'

The guns and knives, my guilt about the kids being taken into care, my hope that one day I'd save Mum as well as myself – the list of reasons was endless. But how can you describe to someone who's never been really afraid about the power fear can have? How can you explain the chains it can clamp around you? I was just a child when The Idiot first hurt me and the seeds of terror he planted were buried so deep that it took years to find the strength to disobey him.

Steven just couldn't understand why I saw Mum and The Idiot. It wasn't often but I sometimes went to visit them or help Michael clean and tidy the flat if there had been complaints from neighbours about the state of it. I'd see Mum then for a few days until the place was a bit straighter before dropping out of touch again for a few weeks or months until I got another phone call to say she needed help or was in hospital. I tried to explain to Steven that although I hated Dad, I still loved Mum and couldn't visit her without seeing him.

But he could not understand, even though I wasn't the only one who behaved like this. Michael hadn't wanted to see Dad all those years ago when we moved back after the kids went into care but did it to give Mum a break. Now he continued to put up with The Idiot for the same reason I did.

Michael had also got back in touch with Laura somehow and told me she was married. No one knew where Kate was because she had been fostered for so long that she had a new family. But our little brother Charlie, who had not been so lucky and spent time in and out of children's homes, chose to stay with Mum and Dad when he came back into our lives. My baby brother was nineteen when I met him again and, just as I'd felt with Simon, it was upsetting to remember how much I'd loved the tiny boy who was now a man I didn't know. Charlie had been in and out of care and was obviously very affected. He couldn't read and reminded me of a child in a man's body.

All of us struggled to deal with the effects of the past in different ways. I think maybe Charlie turned up to see us hoping to somehow make sense of it all but things soon went wrong when he went to live with The Idiot, who wanted to dictate his every move. Charlie, though, had been away long enough to resent Dad's controlling ways and left – disappearing out of our lives for ever after deciding that he didn't want to have anything more to do with his family. Simon had also moved away after leaving my flat and we didn't see too much of him. When Laura got back in touch with Mum and Dad and invited them to stay with her and her husband, The Idiot made trouble there too. I spoke to her occasionally on the phone but our relationship was as damaged as all the others. Meanwhile I knew Michael sometimes drowned his memories with alcohol.

We were all scarred but, like many abused children, couldn't cut all ties with the father who'd hurt us. There are many children who are beaten and burned with cigarettes, betrayed and abused for years, who still want to be with the person who hurt them. A child's love for its parents is a powerful thing and however warped and twisted it is, however abused and trampled on, it often doesn't die.

But I think it was all too much for Steven to understand and his anger only convinced me that no one else ever would. He resented my visits to see Mum and just seemed to get angrier all the time.

We were both to blame for the problems: I couldn't let go of Mum and Steven couldn't bring himself to understand. We argued more and more and soon the doctor put me on tablets to try to help me cope better. I felt so trapped: the more Steven and I argued, the more disobedient the girls became and the more frustrated I got. Soon I found myself shouting at Emma and Lily about tiny things as Steven threw my anger back in my face.

'Have you listened to yourself?' he'd shout. 'Do you want to end up like him?'

I knew there was so much anger inside me and I tried the best I could to control it until a day came when I realised I couldn't cope any more. Emma was being scratchy – I can't remember if she'd tipped her food on to the floor or drawn on the wall – and I felt the anger rush up inside me. But instead of walking out of the room, I picked up the TV remote and hurled it at the wall in frustration. I watched in horror as it bounced off the wall and hit Emma on the leg. She wasn't hurt, just shocked, but as she cried in my arms, I knew I had to do something. Soon afterwards, I contacted social services to ask for help. I told them I wasn't coping and wanted to be a better mother. I was so scared something of Dad was left inside me that I had to act. Would I end up like him? Would I really hurt my girls one day if I lost control? I knew I would die if I did.

I was referred to a counsellor and poured out my story to her.

'So where is your stepfather now?' she asked, and I realised she could not even begin to believe that a biological father would do what mine had done to me.

I put her right but knew it didn't matter whether it was a blood relative or one who had married into my family and hurt me. Children need to be protected and anyone whose job it is to do that can betray them in the worst way possible. The counsellor also asked if I'd considered reporting Dad to the police but I told her I hadn't. If my own husband couldn't understand why I'd stayed locked up in the house where my father had beaten and raped me, then how could a police officer?

I only saw the counsellor for a few sessions before she told me she wasn't experienced enough to deal with someone like me. She said I'd need a whole team of experts and referred me on but I couldn't attend the appointments because they were at 7 p.m., just as I was trying to get the girls into bed, and there was no one else to look after them for me week in week out.

Things did get better in some ways, though, because social services sent someone out to talk to Steven and me. We were told to work as a team but it was really hard. I wanted to discipline the girls, who were getting increasingly wild, but found it difficult to know how to do it properly because I'd never been taught as a child. But I learned one very important thing which was to count to ten whenever I felt angry. I knew I had come close to taking out my temper on the girls and vowed I would never lose control. I wanted to be the best mum I could and however bad things were with Steven, I couldn't bring myself to leave. The Idiot had always told me no one would ever want me. I didn't want my marriage to fail and prove him right so I clung on, hoping against hope that somehow things would get better.

Mum's health was very poor by now and I worried about her a lot but didn't see her regularly until Lily was about two, Emma was three, and she started going in and out of hospital a lot more. Soon I found myself helping out a lot because I knew Dad wouldn't lift a finger to look after her. As my hospital visits increased, so did my trips to see Mum with The Idiot when she was sent home, and I gradually began seeing her several times a week. Steven hated it and wouldn't let me take the girls alone so I'd leave them with him and go to visit for a few hours. I think I used going to see Mum as an escape from the house – even though I knew the comfort I found in seeing her was like a house of cards that could come crashing down any time The Idiot decided he'd had enough of my visits.

But about six months after I started seeing Mum regularly, everything came to a head when Steven and I took the girls to see her and The Idiot was in a foul mood. I could feel it the moment I walked into the lounge and knew he wouldn't be able to hold his tongue for long. Dad looked like thunder as he ordered Mum to get him some tea and when she gave it to him, screamed that it was too hot. She went out to make another cup and as she came back into the room, I saw that her skirt was tucked into her knickers. She must have done it by accident when she went to the toilet and so had no idea why Dad started yelling.

'What the fuck are you playing at?' he raged. 'Have you seen yourself? Are you trying to flash your fanny at Steven, you stupid slag? Do you want him to notice you? Are you trying to get a shag, you whore?'

Mum pulled her skirt free and I got up to help her without a word. I could see Steven's face was still. He was furious.

'It's time to leave,' I said as Mum sat back down again.

'Not too fucking soon either,' The Idiot snarled.

I gathered up the girls before walking to the front door but as we got outside, I could hear Dad shouting at Mum and turned to go back into the flat.

'No!' Steven said. 'Let's get out of here now. I can't stand it any longer.'

I did as he said and worried for the next few days about what had happened when we left. I felt so torn: feeling responsible for Mum but knowing I had to think of my daughters too. I understood why Steven was angry because while Emma and Lily might still be small they'd soon take notice of the abuse my dad dished out. I didn't want them hearing that any more than Steven did but couldn't see a way out.

'What is wrong with you?' he shouted that night. 'Why do you want to keep seeing your mum when he's there?'

'Because I love her. I want to keep an eye on her.'

'Like you wanted to keep her safe when you stayed all those years?' he snapped.

No matter how many times we had the same argument, it still hurt me every time he questioned me. Steven's anger just fed my feelings of guilt and shame.

'I've tried explaining it to you; I don't know what else to say,' I shouted back.

'Explain what? You had a choice, Alice, and you stayed.'

'A choice? He had a gun, Steven, he kept the doors locked, I was sure he'd kill me.'

'So how can you bear seeing him now?'

'Because I have to. I don't want to but I have to if I'm going to see Mum.'

'I don't see why you have to see her at all.'

'Because she's my mum. I love her. She looked after us as kids and kept us safe. I want to do what I can for her.'

'What can you do? It's up to her if she stays.'

'I know, but maybe it might help her to know she's got somewhere to go. I never had that. That was one of the reasons why I stayed so long.'

'Really?'

'What do you mean?'

'Nothing.'

It felt as if he blamed me for staying, as if he thought I'd wanted to be trapped in that house.

I kept my distance from Mum for the next few days as I thought about it all. Could I really stop seeing her? She was so ill and weak, Dad didn't look after her and Michael and

I were the only ones who did. It terrified me to think of abandoning her a second time but seeing her was becoming too much for Steven and me.

A few days later, I got a phone call from The Idiot telling me that Mum had collapsed at home and I left the girls with Steven as I rushed to the flat to find an ambulance parked outside. Running into the living room, I saw Mum collapsed on the end of the bed and Dad lying in it. She wasn't moving and her eyes were closed.

'Mum!' I cried as I rushed towards her.

Had he killed her this time? She was white as a sheet and so still.

'She's unconscious,' a paramedic told me as another strapped an oxygen mask to her face. 'She's very poorly. We need to get her to hospital as quickly as possible.'

'What?' I whispered as my stomach turned over.

I couldn't lose Mum. I couldn't bear her to leave me. Not like this. Not here with him looking on and sneering at her.

'Can't you get her off this bed?' The Idiot snarled. 'She didn't even make my fucking breakfast and I'm diabetic.'

I felt sick as I heard him speak.

'I don't think she was well enough to do it,' the paramedic said coldly.

When Mum was finally put into the ambulance, Dad refused to get out of his bed to go with her to hospital.

'I'm too ill,' he snapped, and I left him lying where he was.

He disgusted me beyond words.

When I arrived at the hospital, the doctors told me Mum was critically ill and they didn't know if she would survive the night. Apparently she'd stopped breathing but they'd managed to bring her back.

'Your mother is very sick,' a doctor said. 'What would you like us to do, Alice, if she stops breathing again?'

My legs felt weak as I heard those words but I knew what I had to say.

'Let her go in peace,' I replied.

I could give Mum that if nothing else.

She was unconscious for thirty-six hours until she came round again but I didn't see her when she did. When The Idiot found out what I'd said to the doctors, he forbade me from seeing her and told them that Mum should be revived if anything happened to her. No matter how much she suffered, he wanted her brought back.

But even if he hadn't stopped me from seeing her, I knew things couldn't go on as they had. If I did not show Steven that he and the girls meant more to me than anything else in the world then I might lose him. He had to know he was everything to me and, however much I didn't want to do it, I knew I'd have to leave Mum a second time to try to save myself.

CHAPTER TWENTY-SEVEN

'Do you want another drink, Alice?' Steven's sister Donna said as she held up a bottle.

I was at Donna's house for a night with some of her girl-friends and was pleased to have been invited. I hadn't got on all that well with her when we first met because Donna thought I was too old for her brother and, thanks to the dowdy clothes I wore when I was first free, I had to admit that I'd probably looked it. But Donna and I had learned to get on better and I was also fond of Steven's mum, Joan.

Tonight Donna had got a fortune teller round for the evening for a bit of fun. Her friends were all laughing as they went into a bedroom one by one before coming out and telling each other what their future held.

'I'm going to get married and have a family,' one told us excitedly.

'And I'm going to get a good job,' exclaimed another.

Donna's friends obviously all loved the idea of finding out about what was going to happen to them but it scared me. Emma was nearly five, Lily was three-and-a-half and things between Steven and me were as bad as ever. I'd hardly seen Mum since the day she collapsed more than a year before but it hadn't made the difference to my relationship with Steven that I'd hoped it would. Things were still so bad that I worried we'd never work it out. Neither of us, though, was ready to be the one to finally give up on our family.

Sometimes I lay awake at night as I tried to make sense of it all. I'd got married believing so strongly that it would be for ever. All I wanted was a normal life but it had fallen apart. I felt as if my own husband hated me and knew the situation was affecting the girls because children pick up on what's in the air around them. I wanted them to feel safe and happy but it was as if I was in a tunnel and there wasn't an escape. I knew I'd made mistakes and it was hard for Steven to understand why I'd kept in touch with Mum but I couldn't find any more ways to explain it and he could not forget.

'Are you going to go in to see the fortune teller?' a woman asked as she stood next to me. 'It's good fun.'

'I'm not sure,' I said. 'It's not really my kind of thing. I don't believe in all that.'

'Oh, go on,' she replied. 'You should have a go. You never know what you might discover!'

As other people went in, I thought about what the woman had said. She was right. I should do just what everyone else was doing – treat it like a bit of fun and take whatever was said with a pinch of salt.

I walked into the bedroom to find a woman with long streaky blonde hair sitting in a chair. I did not know what I'd expected but she wasn't it – she looked so normal. But even so I started shaking as I sat down opposite her.

'Can I see your hand?' the woman asked, and I held it out. She looked at it closely for a few seconds before speaking. 'You have three children.'

'No.'

'I see a little boy.'

'No. I have two girls.'

The woman looked at me.

'But you've lost a baby?'

I wanted to pull my hand away, stop her seeing these things. Did she know about Jonathan?

'Yes,' I said quietly.

The woman's eyes looked sad as she lowered them to examine my hand again.

'The baby you lost – was its conception out of the ordinary?'

I gasped as she spoke.

'Was it someone close to you?' the woman asked softly.

I pulled my hand away.

'What do you mean?' I exclaimed. 'I thought this was supposed to be a bit of fun. I don't know what you're talking about.'

In all this time, I'd only ever told Steven and the counsellor about what had happened and now this woman had seen my secrets. She didn't speak as I struggled to get my feelings under control. I could hear Donna's friends laughing and chatting. I wanted to run back to them and forget this.

'You know you can still get something done about it.' The fortune teller spoke slowly as if she was choosing her words carefully. 'You can still get him charged.'

'What?' I gasped.

'I understand what happened to you. I can see it in your palm.'

'Please stop,' I pleaded. 'I don't know what you're talking about.'

The fortune teller looked at me with sadness in her eyes.

'I know how you feel, Alice,' she said.

'What do you mean?' I whispered.

'I was abused by someone close to me just like you.'

I couldn't speak as she leaned towards me. How did the woman know these things?

'I got the man who hurt me charged for it fifteen years later,' she said. 'He was locked up for what he did. You could do the same.'

Her voice was quiet as she spoke.

'Tell me what happened to you.'

One minute I wanted to run but the next my secrets were spilling out of me. I didn't know why but somehow I knew I could trust this woman. I'd never met someone who'd been abused before and I started crying as the fortune teller asked me questions about what had happened. Slowly I told her my story and described everything – the start, the birth of Jonathan and the death of Caitlin. I felt exhausted when I finally finished speaking.

'You can do it, you know,' the woman told me.

'Do what? It's all in the past. It's forgotten. Anyway, the police wouldn't believe me.'

'They would,' she replied. 'I know they would because I did what you are going to do.'

'What?' I gasped. 'You mean actually go to the police? I couldn't. I'm too scared.'

'You're stronger than you know, Alice.'

I could hardly take in what she was saying. Go to the police? Dredge everything back up that I was trying so hard to forget?

'I can't do it,' I sobbed.

'Yes, you can. You have to, Alice. You deserve justice.'

I stumbled out of the room and back to where Donna's friends were still laughing and chatting.

'How did you get on?' Joan asked as I walked in.

I was silent as the fortune teller's words rang in my ears.

Could I really do what she had said? Was I really ready for that?

'I could still get him charged,' I gasped as I looked at Joan.

The women around me stopped talking as I stood shaking, my mind racing.

'What do you mean?' Joan asked.

I looked up at her, suddenly remembering where I was and who I was with.

'Nothing,' I said. 'I'm sorry. Don't listen to me. I don't know what I'm saying.'

But I couldn't forget what the fortune teller had told me after I got home. Could I really go to the police after all this time? The idea frightened me but as the days passed I realised that I might be finally ready to hear the message I had been given. I'd never thought properly about going to the police because of what had happened when the kids were taken and Jonathan was born all those years ago. They'd wanted to help me then but I'd refused and I'd always thought they would never listen to me again. But the more I thought about it, the more I knew the fortune teller was right. I would never put the past behind me if I did not confront it.

I'd spent so long running and where had it got me? I was on medication for depression, my marriage was crumbling and I longed to be a better mum – and all because a river of poison inside kept drowning me. I had flashbacks and bad dreams; the feelings of shame and worthlessness were as strong as they had been when I was a girl and my father touched me for the first time. I'd run from The Idiot but he was still controlling me: frightening me in my dreams and refusing to allow me to see Mum. I was almost as scared of him as I ever had been. I had to do something. It was time

for it to end. I must try at least – however frightened I was.
I had to do something for myself instead of running.

My courage failed me a dozen times when I looked up the
number of the local police station and went to dial it. My fingers froze as I picked up the phone and I couldn't bring
myself to carry on. Steven had said he'd stick by me if I
reported Dad and I knew it was what he wanted. I wondered
if maybe it would finally show him that however much my
past was still dragging me down, I loved him and the girls
more than anything. But I just couldn't pick up the phone. I
was too scared. By the time the weekend arrived, I was still
turning it all over in my mind when Steven and I took the
girls to visit Joan. Donna was with her when we arrived and
Joan shooed Steven out of the house with Emma and Lily.

'Take them to the shops and get them a treat,' she told
him. 'I want to speak to Alice.'

Joan, Donna and I were left alone and we got a cup of tea
before sitting down in the lounge. I knew what Joan wanted
to talk about – the fortune teller. Everyone had noticed
how upset I was after seeing her.

'I'm going to ask you something and I want you to tell
me the truth,' Joan said.

'Okay,' I replied uncertainly.

'You've told me about your miscarriages and Jonathan
and Caitlin.'

'Yes.'

'But I've always known something wasn't right, Alice,
and what you said at the fortune teller's convinced me.'

I gulped my tea and waited for her to speak again.

'I don't want you to be scared but there is something I
need to ask you,' said Joan. 'Did your father hurt you? Was
he your babies' father too?'

I couldn't believe Joan had said it, spoken the words as if

they were believable. I didn't know what to say.

'You can tell us, Alice. Donna and I want to help you.'

I stared at them.

'Yes,' I whispered.

Joan got up to hug me as I started to cry. Neither of us spoke until eventually I stopped crying and Joan turned to me again.

'Why did you never tell us, Alice?' she asked kindly. 'We would have helped you.'

'Because I wanted to get away from it, have a normal life like everyone else. I wanted to forget.'

'But how can you do that without help?'

'I don't know,' I cried. 'Steven said he'd help me.'

Joan looked at me silently for a moment. I knew now that Steven wasn't going to do that. He was too young to cope with all this and too disgusted by what had happened to me to see past it.

'So what are you going to do?' Joan asked.

'I don't know.'

'I think you do, Alice.'

Joan stood up and got out the phone book from under the telephone. She copied down a number and handed it to me.

Later that afternoon, after Steven and I had got home and the girls were playing, I picked up the phone and dialled the number Joan had given me. It was for the local police station.

My heart hammered as the phone rung.

'CID,' a voice said, and I took a deep breath.

'I want to report a crime,' I replied.

CHAPTER TWENTY-EIGHT

I almost backed out a thousand times when I knew an officer was going to come and see me. I couldn't believe I'd actually made the phone call and felt terrified when there was a knock on the door a couple of days later.

'I'm Detective Constable Patrick O'Mara,' an officer said as I invited him in. 'I'm here to talk about the crime you reported. This is my colleague Susan.'

I could tell immediately that Patrick was a kind man. He had that look about him – tall with dark hair, he seemed open and friendly.

'Would you like a cup of tea?' I asked nervously.

'Sure,' Patrick said.

It felt so unreal that the police were actually in my house and I wondered where I was going to begin.

'At the beginning,' Patrick said when I asked him. 'Take us right back to when you were a little girl and tell us what you remember. We've got as much time as you need.'

So I started speaking and the words tumbled out of me. Patrick asked some questions but mostly he let me talk and didn't look shocked or disgusted – he had the same calm look on his face throughout everything I said.

When I finally finished, I had just one question of my own that I wanted to ask Patrick.

'Do you believe what I'm saying?'

'Yes,' he replied.

After that first meeting, I had to go down to the police station to be formally interviewed by Patrick and it took two days to take my statement. It was very hard going through everything because I had to give details that I'd never spoken about before. I knew it was necessary but there were moments when I could see the shock on Patrick's face and it made me wonder what other people would think about what had happened to me. I realised other women had been abused as children but was sure I must be the only one whose father had forced the worst possible sin on her. It was disgusting and I felt embarrassed talking about it but Patrick never once made me feel uncomfortable. He listened to me and that was what mattered.

'I'll be the one investigating your complaint, Alice,' he told me. 'But it could take some time. There are medical records to go through, social services reports to obtain and maybe laboratory tests to run. We have to be sure we can get enough evidence to charge anyone with a crime and that takes a while.'

In the months that followed, I rang Patrick regularly to get updates on what was happening. I knew he was working as hard as possible, talking to hospitals and social services, schools and police. I just hoped he'd be able to find enough evidence because in cases like mine – where the crime happened many years ago and was hidden from everyone – it was difficult. The specific details of events I had provided helped, of course, but there was little else to back up my story because I had been so hidden from everyone; for instance, I hadn't seen my doctor during one pregnancy because I'd miscarried so early and had given a false name when I attended hospital for another. Even the four pregnancies on my medical records weren't proof that my father had abused me. There was just one thing that would prove him guilty beyond all reasonable doubt – physical evidence. But would Patrick get it?

I prayed he would find what he needed and worried about the case continually. Had I done the right thing? Would The Idiot be made to pay? And what would he do to me or Mum if he was? I was in no doubt that Dad might try to take revenge and the thought made me shudder. I also felt petrified of the truth coming out because I'd hidden it for so long and wasn't sure if I could bear people knowing. But I just kept telling myself that I'd done the right thing. I'd done what I had to do and I was going to finally finish what Dad had started more than two decades before. It had been six years since I'd run away and now I was finally strong enough to stand up to him.

Steven was relieved when I first went to the police. But as the months went on, things slipped back to how they'd been for so long. I sometimes wondered if I should ever have gone to the police. Would it really be worth it if it didn't make the difference to my marriage that I'd hoped it would and Patrick didn't find enough evidence? Then I'd have been through all this for nothing.

I didn't want anyone to know that I'd been to the police but a few weeks later Steven and I went to visit Michael and Julie. I left the two men in the lounge as I chatted to Julie in the kitchen but a few minutes later I heard Michael calling me.

'What's going on, Alice?' he asked as I went in to see him.

'What do you mean?'

'Steven's told me everything,' Michael snapped.

'Told you what?'

'About what that fucking arsehole did to you.'

Michael sounded really angry. I couldn't believe that Steven had told him. I didn't want anyone knowing because I wasn't even sure if Dad would get charged or not. When I knew one way or the other then I'd decide what to do about telling people, but not now.

'Why did you tell him?' I shouted at Steven. 'You had no right.'

'Why didn't you tell me?' Michael yelled back. 'I can't believe you kept this secret. We took you in. You must have known you could have talked to us.'

'No! I thought you'd kick me out if you knew.'

'What?' Michael roared. 'I would never have done that. You're my kid sister. You should have told me. I could have helped. I never had a clue, Alice. I really didn't.'

'I know,' I said.

Suddenly I could see that Michael wasn't angry – he was upset. He never really showed how he felt but his eyes blazed as he looked at me, just as they had when he was young and Dad had taunted him.

'I would have dealt with it,' he said quietly.

'And got locked up?' I cried. 'You know what he's like and I knew he'd punish all of you even more if I said a word.'

'But what about that time I came to visit you when you were pregnant with Jonathan? I asked you then if what the police were saying was true and you said it wasn't. I believed you, Alice. I never imagined . . .'

'No one did and I didn't want you getting into trouble.'

'I wouldn't have cared!' Michael cried. 'At least you'd have got away.'

'He'd have killed you. Don't you remember the weapons, Michael? The knives he had?'

Michael was silent as I spoke. I knew he was remembering the things he'd seen – snatches of memories which somehow now made sense: why I'd suddenly become so withdrawn when I was young; why I'd hidden myself away for hours on end; why I'd wanted so desperately to run away with him.

'I'm sorry, Alice,' he kept repeating. 'You should have told me.'

We looked at each other for a moment.

'Maybe he'll finally get what he deserves,' I said quietly.

'I hope so,' my brother replied.

After that day, Michael and I spoke a few times about the police investigation but not often. I knew he felt terribly guilty about what had happened and blamed himself. He was tortured by the fact that he'd left me with The Idiot and, however much I tried to tell him that it wasn't his fault, he didn't believe me. It made me sad that Michael was hurting again and in a way I wished he didn't know. I didn't want to cause him any more pain because he had done nothing wrong and although it was hard telling strangers about what had happened, it felt even more difficult to tell the people I loved like Michael because I was worried they might judge me as Steven had.

But Michael and Julie were as kind as ever and I told myself that if I wanted to see the police investigation through then I would have to be prepared for people to know everything about me. It was hard but it would be worth it if The Idiot was made to pay for what he'd done. That was all I could think about as a new feeling filled me – anger. Over and over, I imagined Dad opening the door to find a police officer waiting and, as much as I wanted the moment for myself, I also wanted it for Mum.

I'd seen her just once since her collapse more than a year before and being apart from her had made me realise Mum would never leave Dad on her own. But I hoped it might help her if The Idiot was charged with a crime and everything was dragged into the open. I was scared, of course, about what Mum might feel but also wondered if it would be what she needed to finally break free. Dad had stolen so much from both of us and, when I felt weak, the thought of Mum helped me keep going with the police complaint. I had to try to save her.

The months passed and the investigation continued. Patrick hoped my allegations might be proved by DNA evidence and had enquired about exhuming Jonathan's body. But he'd been told it would be impossible because my son had been buried in a public plot near the hospital with other stillborn babies. It made me so sad to discover that and remember I hadn't even been allowed to say goodbye to Jonathan.

That was the part of the investigation I found most difficult and it upset me greatly to think about losing Jonathan and Caitlin again. I didn't want them to be disturbed after all this time. But Patrick had to investigate every possible avenue and I accepted it was what he would have to do if I wanted The Idiot to be charged.

Caitlin had been cremated but Patrick told me he hoped tissue samples kept during her post-mortem and suspended in paraffin blocks for all these years might give him what he needed for the investigation. In January 2005, nine months after I went to the police, small pieces of the samples were sent to a forensics laboratory for the DNA to be extracted.

In the same month, Dad was held as a suspect and DNA samples were taken from him.

All I could do was wait and the weeks slid by as I wondered what was going to happen. It was early May when the phone finally rang. It was Patrick.

'I have some important news,' he said.

I held my breath.

'The DNA tests have shown that your father was Caitlin's biological father. They prove your story, Alice.'

'Really?' I whispered.

I'd always known the tests would prove Caitlin's paternity but it was still a shock to hear it. The words hit me when Patrick said them. Finally, the world would know what The Idiot had done, the sickness at the heart of him, the lives he'd ruined. There was no way now he could escape being punished.

'So what happens now?' I asked.

'We're going to charge your father with incest.'

CHAPTER TWENTY-NINE

I'd known all along that The Idiot would have laughed at the police even when he was getting arrested and his DNA sample was being taken. But now he was going to be charged, I was sure even he couldn't think it was still a joke. The thought terrified me all over again and I started looking over my shoulder as I worried that somehow he'd try to hurt Emma and Lily. I knew he didn't have a shred of conscience about hurting me and feared he'd do anything to get back at me through the girls or Mum now he knew that I had finally told our secrets.

I took comfort from the fact that he'd be locked up in prison but was wrong to think someone charged with a crime like my father's would be held before his trial. He was set free after being charged because Patrick told me the crimes related to events so many years ago that The Idiot wasn't considered a possible threat to the public any more. I just had to wait for the case to come to trial, which could take months because courts were busy places, lawyers had to build their cases and things moved forward very slowly. Once again, all I could do was wait and the thought of Dad being out there somewhere terrified me. I heard rumours that he was threatening to do something – whispers that he was planning to snatch Emma from school and take her away. Part of me knew it was another empty threat but I was also scared he'd been pushed over the edge and started taking Emma all the way into the school building instead of leaving her at the gate and refusing to let her and Lily outside to play. I did not want to suffocate the girls but it was hard not to because I knew of all the dangers that could be waiting for them.

Patrick told me The Idiot was stunned when he was charged and denied everything. It was like torture. I just wanted the case to get to court and felt more and more petrified. Dad being charged hadn't helped the situation with Steven and I feared I might lose what little strength I had left if something did not happen soon. I was on the edge all the time and there just didn't seem to be a way back for Steven and me now – a wedge had been driven between us by my past.

'I suppose you're going to drop the charges now and let him get away with it?' he'd yell when I told him how scared I was that Dad might try to do something.

'No!' I'd cry. 'I've come this far. I'm not going to give up now.'

But inside I wondered if I should. The thought of getting up in court and facing Dad was almost more than I could bear. I kept imagining it over and over again: him staring at me as I gave evidence; the sneer on his face as I told the world about what he'd done. I'd heard enough whispers from his relatives to know he was still insisting that I was a lying bastard. I'd been stupid to think he might finally realise the law was catching up with him – he was so arrogant that he'd never do the decent thing and admit his guilt. The Idiot didn't care and believed he'd get away with it if he lied enough – just as he had done all those years before when the kids were taken.

I saw him once just after he was charged. I hadn't seen Mum for months and was desperate to because I knew her health was even worse. I had to risk trying to see her when I heard she'd been admitted to hospital again. I wouldn't forgive myself if I lost her.

I went to the hospital and felt sick to my stomach as I walked on to the ward. I could see Michael, Simon and Sam by the bed and Dad, just as he always was, like a spider waiting in the shadows. Two of his relatives were also there.

'What are you doing here, you little slag?' one screamed as soon as they saw me. 'You're not fucking welcome, you lying bitch.'

People stared as I walked towards Mum. I knew I had to look brave even if I didn't feel it. Michael was here. He'd look after me. The Idiot's eyes bored into me as I went up to the bed.

'Hi, Mum,' I said as I held out a photo of the girls.

She hadn't seen them in a long time.

'They're getting big, aren't they?' she said as she looked at the picture and smiled.

'Yes. I'll leave it for you so you can have a better look later.'

Mum's eyes were lifeless and her skin pale. She looked so sick. Her heart and weight problems were getting too much for her. I laid the photo on the cabinet beside her bed and she reached out to pick it up.

'Give it back,' The Idiot spat.

His words jolted through me but he didn't turn his eyes to look at me. He just stared at Mum as if I wasn't there until she held out the photo in her hand. I could see she was scared.

'It's only a picture,' I cried, feeling tears welling up inside, but The Idiot just ignored me as I spoke.

There was no point in staying. I'd given Mum what I wanted to and couldn't stand being there with him watching. But as I bent down to give her a kiss goodbye, she whispered in my ear: 'Don't go.' Michael, Simon, Sam and I left the ward and I found a family room to hide in. I couldn't go without seeing Mum again and waited until visiting hours were over and I knew Dad had gone. I felt weak and shaky from just being in the same place as him.

'How have you been?' Mum asked as I sat down beside her.

'Not so good.'

I knew I had to stop myself from crying. I must be strong and show her that I had done the right thing by going to the police. Then maybe she'd see it could all end for her too. The truth was finally coming out now.

'Why are you doing this?' Mum asked.

'Because I have to. I'll never be free otherwise.'

I knew Mum was too weak to say any more. She didn't have the strength to find the words to start speaking about the court case because it would mean talking about what we'd never admitted to each other. I didn't try to push her and Mum didn't say any more about the police investigation as we chatted for a few minutes before a nurse came to check on her and I had to leave. I understood why Mum didn't ask more about Dad: it had taken me years to break free and start talking about it. In time we might talk but not now.

All I could hope was that Dad would be jailed and Mum could finally begin to see life without him. I would show her that she deserved some happiness as soon as he was locked away. I just had to keep my faith that it would finally be over when Dad was brought into court. The DNA evidence proved he was Caitlin's father and surely even he wasn't stupid enough to think he could argue himself out of that?

But, of course, my father tried to escape the law once he finally realised it was turning against him. Before a trial, there are various hearings to deal with different legal matters and one was set for summer 2005. But Patrick phoned to say Dad had not attended. He'd disappeared with Mum and no one knew where he was – or if they did they were hiding him. The Idiot would do anything he could to avoid being made to pay – even if it meant going on the run from the law. But it meant I knew one important thing now: finally he was the one who was scared.

Steven sat down beside me.

'We're doing the right thing, aren't we?' he asked.

'Yes,' I replied. 'I think we are.'

The atmosphere was strained between us as we discussed our separation. We'd both finally accepted the mistakes we'd made would never be mended and had agreed that for everyone's sake we would soon start living apart. We had been married for six-and-a-half years and all the hopes we'd both had were finally gone.

'I've tried so hard to make a go of things but I can't do it alone,' I told Steven. 'I stopped seeing Mum and concentrated on you and the girls but it hasn't made a difference. It's all gone too far.'

It was December 2005 and Steven and I had decided that he would move out once we'd had Christmas with Emma and Lily. I felt sad but had finally accepted that we would never make things work. However much of a failure I felt, I knew it was not doing the girls any good to live in such an unhappy house. I wanted to give them a more solid base to build on – even if it meant doing it alone. Steven would live nearby and see them regularly while I'd stay in our flat with Emma and Lily. I wished he'd say sorry or admit that it wasn't all my fault but Steven still blamed my family for everything that had gone wrong.

'I'll start packing my things,' he said as he got up to walk away from me.

We made the decision very calmly and I was pleased we could do one thing right after all the years of arguing. But the situation took a turn for the worse just before Christmas when Steven discovered I'd made a friend whom I could talk to. I'd met a man called Nick through one of the mums at Emma's school and, although there was nothing between us but friendship, I'd poured out my troubles to him – the police case, the situation with Steven and the worries I had about whether I was doing the right thing. It seemed like years since I'd had anyone who actually listened to me and Nick let me talk as much as I wanted to as we chatted on the phone. Being in a bad relationship was very lonely. Suddenly there was someone to talk to who at least tried to understand what I was going through and I took comfort from that.

But my friendship with Nick caused a lot of bad feeling with Steven and his family when they found out about it and accused me of having an affair. Although I knew Nick and I had done nothing wrong, it upset me a great deal because I'd once been close to Joan and Donna and they'd supported me through the long police investigation. Now everyone seemed so angry and, alone with the girls, I felt very down at times. Michael lived quite a distance away now so I didn't see too much of him but we spoke regularly on the phone and my nieces Paula and Jacqueline came to visit. My cousin Sam also kept an eye on me and it was good to have him and my other cousins around because it made me feel safer.

I carried on seeing Nick as a friend once Steven had

moved out and a couple of months later things went further with him. Weeks later I found out I was pregnant again. I was in such a mess that I'd taken a chance with Nick and couldn't believe I was having another baby when I'd just become a single mum. How would I cope with another child? I'd been so stupid to let this happen. But after thinking long and hard about whether to carry on with the pregnancy, I knew I had to. The miscarriages I'd had in the past still deeply affected me and there was no way I could intentionally stop a life growing inside me. Besides, it wasn't the baby's fault and I wanted to keep it however difficult a time it was for me.

I knew what I wanted to do but also felt there was no way I could jump into another full-time relationship. I wanted to carry on seeing Nick if that was what he wanted too but I was going to take the baby home alone when I had it. I still felt so hurt by all that had happened with Steven. I'd believed in him and our marriage so strongly and I'd failed. I wasn't ready to commit to someone else again and be hurt but I knew my baby deserved to know its dad and Nick was a good man. I told him how I felt and let the girls know they were soon going to have a little brother or sister.

At night, I'd lie in bed wondering how on earth it would all end. I was pregnant, alone and my father was out there somewhere laughing at me and the law – just as he'd always done. I had no idea where he was but sometimes I felt sure I could feel him watching me as coldness crept down my spine and I whirled around to an empty room. It was just my mind playing tricks, of course, but it felt more real to me the longer time dragged on and I waited for the police to finally catch up with him.

CHAPTER THIRTY

It wasn't long after I found out I was pregnant that Michael told me Mum had been taken into hospital again. He didn't know where The Idiot was but had heard she was ill from a relative. I knew the police had been making enquiries trying to find Dad but so far they hadn't been able to because while the case might have felt like the most important thing in the world to me, it was just one of many for them. There was only so much time and money they could put into trying to find my father.

It was 2006 and Mum hadn't seen the girls for nearly three years so I collected them from school and took them up to the hospital. But as I walked into the entrance hall, the lift doors opened and I saw a glimpse of a familiar figure. I prayed The Idiot wouldn't see us as I pulled the girls into the hospital café and sat down at a table with my back to the windows. Cowering behind a wall, I knew I needed to tell the police as soon as I could that he was still in this city. But I couldn't face him. I wasn't strong enough. I just wanted to see Mum.

'What's wrong?' Emma asked as I sat still, holding my breath.

'Nothing, darling,' I said.

Pulling the girls to me, I cuddled them until I knew The Idiot must have left before going to find Mum. She was lying still in bed as we walked into the ward – an oxygen mask on her face and dark shadows under her eyes. She couldn't take her eyes off us as I walked towards her bed with Emma and Lily. I gently pushed them in front of me so she could see them better as the three of us stood by the bed.

'Hello, Mum,' I said softly.

It was so long since I'd last seen her and I wanted to cry as I looked at her. I bent down to hug her and she put her arm around me. I could see her trying to smile underneath the mask as I stood back up.

'It's so good to see you,' I said.

As the girls turned away to start chattering to the person in the next bed, I leaned in to speak to Mum.

'Why don't you move in with me when you're discharged from here? Please, Mum. I can make you comfortable. Look after you. Make sure you get the right medication and see the nurses.'

Her eyes flickered as I spoke. She was drowsy and I could see it was hard for her to stay awake. Her hand tightened on mine as she opened her eyes a little more.

'The only way I'm going to get away from him is if I die,' she whispered.

'But it should be him who dies!' I cried. 'Not you.'

Mum's eyes shut again and her hand slackened on mine.

'I'll come back tomorrow,' I said softly as I bent to kiss her forehead.

It felt as if my heart was breaking as I left her that day. I had to find a way to convince her to come and stay with us. I couldn't let The Idiot intimidate me. I'd tell the police I had seen him and they'd arrest him. If there was one thing I could give to Mum it was a bit of dignity and comfort in her last days. I rang Patrick and woke up the next morning determined to somehow persuade Mum to join me. I knew I'd find a way. I had to. But when I got back up to the hospital, I walked towards her bed to find it empty.

'Where is she?' I asked a nurse as I stared at it.

'Didn't you know?' she replied. 'Your mother was discharged this morning. She's left.'

'But wasn't she was supposed to be here for another few days?'

'She wanted to go home and the doctor said she was well enough.'

I couldn't believe she'd had the strength to walk out of the hospital but knew who'd ordered her to – The Idiot. Once more they'd disappeared and it would be months before I got any news of Mum. I thought of her all the time as I wondered where and how she was. The Idiot did not care what he did to her and I worried that soon whatever strength she had left would fail. I prayed that the police would catch up with him in time to help her.

But on Christmas Day 2006, I was holding my one-month-old son Tom as I got the girls ready to go to Steven's for the day and the phone rang. I picked it up to hear Michael's voice on the other end. It was so quiet.

'Alice?' he said.

'Yes.'

'I've got some bad news.'

'What's happened?'

'Mum is dead.'

I felt the ground fall away beneath me as I staggered. Nick, who was there with me, took Tom from me as I dropped the phone. I couldn't believe it. Mum had gone?

Now I'd never get her away from the Idiot, she'd never be free.

'He says there's no way any of us are going to Mum's funeral,' Michael told me a few days later.

We still didn't know where The Idiot was but we were getting messages via his relatives. Michael had been told that even though he, Simon and I all wanted to attend the funeral, we weren't going to be allowed to. We were dead to our mother. We weren't her children.

'But he's got to let us say goodbye!' I cried. 'Even he can't stop us doing that.'

For the next couple of days, messages went back and forth between Michael and Dad's relatives until we were finally told that Dad had agreed to let us attend the funeral on one condition – I had to promise not to cause any trouble.

'They want your word that you won't get him arrested at the funeral,' Michael told me.

I should have known that Dad's relatives would side with him and believe the lies he told. He was one of their own and they'd protect him.

'Of course, I won't,' I told my brother. 'I wouldn't do anything to ruin Mum's funeral.'

But the phone calls were enough to help me work out that Dad was staying with a relative. That's where he was hiding out, hoping that somehow the police would forget everything if he stayed out of sight for long enough. It was the first time I'd known where he was since he disappeared and I wondered for a moment if I really had the courage to get him arrested before Mum's funeral. It would be the ultimate act of revenge that he would never forget but I knew I had to do it for her sake and mine. I'd assured everyone that I wouldn't make trouble on the day but hadn't made a promise about any other time.

'I know where he is,' I said when I phoned Patrick.

I gave him the address and sat back to wait. The next day Patrick phoned me. Dad had been arrested and was being held in custody. He'd be held until he attended court and then released again but this time the police would keep close tabs on him to make sure he couldn't run. He'd have to face justice now. It was too late for Mum but at last he knew that I would not stop until I saw him in court. However scared I felt, I was determined to see this through.

Of course The Idiot's family went wild and we were immediately told that none of us could go to the funeral. I was a lying slag, a troublemaker and a fantasist. Why was I making this up when Dad had just lost his wife? I felt almost sorry that they still believed his lies but also disgusted they could even consider I'd make anything up like that. Why would I go to the police and go through all I had – the statement, the waiting, the tests and fear – for nothing?

Michael was told there'd be a viewing of Mum's body the day before her funeral which he and Simon could attend if they wanted to. But he was told by my Dad's relatives that there was no way I could show my face. I was not going to be allowed to take one step over the threshold of where Mum's body lay. There was no way I could say goodbye after what I'd done.

'I've had enough of this,' Michael said. 'You're coming with me now he's out of the way. You've more right to be there than any of them.'

I left the girls and Tom with Nick and drove up to the funeral parlour. I was shaking as I walked in with Michael.

I felt numb inside. I couldn't believe Mum had gone, that this was the last time I'd ever see her. If only I'd gone to the police sooner maybe I'd have been able to get her away.

As we walked in Dad's relatives were crowded in the room where Mum's body was laid out. I tensed up as I waited for their abuse but they just looked at me with hate in their eyes before turning to leave.

Now it was just Michael, Simon and me – the remains of our family, the boys I'd sat with on a bed when we were children and imagined a future full of fun and feasts when we finally escaped our father. How differently our lives had turned out. In one way or another all of us had never really escaped him. My brothers stood either side of me as we looked down at Mum. She was so thin and pale, not as I remembered her when we were young: chubby and bright-eyed, full of laughter as she'd twirled us around the living room to music. The room was silent as I took her hand and kissed her cold fingers.

'I'm sorry I couldn't get you away,' I whispered.

But as I looked at Mum's face I realised something: she might not have escaped Dad in life but now at last she was free. He was finally going to be made to face what he'd done and Mum's pain was over for ever. She was at peace now and soon I would be too. I was going to get justice. My torturer was going to pay. He would finally know what it felt like to be locked up in a prison.

EPILOGUE

I didn't have to face the ordeal of giving evidence at a trial because my father pleaded guilty to incest and was sentenced to three years in jail. I felt disappointed that he'd serve such a short time but that was the sentence the judge gave him and I had to accept it. The incest charge related to Caitlin's conception and was just the tip of the iceberg of what The Idiot had done to me. But because everything had happened so long ago, it would have been a case of my word against his and the authorities decided to go with the one crime they could prove. The judge in the case also had to take into account the fact that Dad had pleaded guilty, which meant he got a shorter sentence.

It was hard to understand but I also knew that three years would be a long time in jail for a sex offender. Finally it was over and as he sat in his prison cell, my father would know I was the one who'd gone to the police and turned him in. I'd shown him that I wasn't scared of him any more and I knew it was time for my life to finally begin again. Getting justice isn't simply about courts and prison sentences; it is also about taking back some of the power that has been stripped away from you and showing your abuser that you are finally ready to stand up to them and break the silence. That is what I had done at last: I had reported my father to the police and when he had gone on the run, I'd helped them track him down. I had shown him that I would not be afraid any more and that was just as important to me as any court case.

In the months that followed, I concentrated on bringing up Emma and Lily, watching Tom grow and being a mother. Steven still saw the girls, Nick was very involved with Tom and I was proud that somehow we'd all found a way to make things work. I often wondered, though, what I would tell my children in the future because I was as sure as ever that my ordeal was unique and I was scared of them ever knowing about what had happened to me. But I realised I was not alone when the crimes of Josef Fritzl made worldwide news in April 2008.

Until then, I'd had no idea other women had gone through similar experiences to mine. But after the discovery of Fritzl's daughter Elisabeth and her children in an Austrian cellar, several cases appeared in the newspapers about other women who'd been forced to have their father's children. Each one was truly terrible but they made me realise I wasn't alone. I wasn't the only daughter to be trapped for years in an abusive situation or the only one who took a long time to finally confess to what had happened and ask for help. At least I had been able to escape because my father's prison was more psychological than physical. Josef Fritzl had locked his daughter in a basement and my heart went out to her unimaginable suffering – and that of her children.

It was then that I decided to tell my story because I knew I would be content if just one woman like me found comfort in it and maybe the courage to speak out. The worst thing about abuse is the secrecy and isolation it feeds on. I always believed I had done something truly awful to deserve what happened to me — that sense of self-hatred was ground into me and it was only when I finally went to the police that I began to move past it. It's very hard: life isn't neat and my past will always be part of me. But I only have to look at my children to know that I have achieved something. Emma and Lily are lively, affectionate and bright little girls while Tom is an energetic toddler. When I look at them, I know I have done one good thing in my life. My father did everything he could to destroy me and make me his prisoner for ever. But I found my courage, fought back and now I have three beautiful children and a life with them. It is more than I ever hoped for. It is the best proof possible that he will not control me in the future as he once did in the past. I am finally free.